GENDER, SCIENCE AND TECHNOLOGY:

INSERVICE HANDBOOK

Judith Whyte

Longman

This title, an outcome of work done for the Schools Council
before its closure, is published under the aegis of the
School Curriculum Development Committee, Newcombe House,
45 Notting Hill Gate, London W11 3JB.

Published by Longman
Longman Resources Unit
62 Hallfield Road
York
YO3 7XQ

# CONTENTS

## Note on contents

This handbook is divided into three units corresponding with the informational, attitudinal and practical elements considered at the GIST teacher workshops. Each unit provides guidance notes for tutors on presentation, and there are nine 'lecturettes' which can be used as the basis for introductory talks to the group. Units I and II also contain notes and resources for nine workshop activities and in Unit III six resource ideas to help teachers carry out their own interventions in the classroom.

# INTRODUCTION

The purpose of this handbook is to give ideas and practical help to those wishing to run courses or workshops for teachers of science and technology who are concerned with the under-representation of girls in their subjects. It should assist those concerned with the in-service education of teachers - local authority advisers, headteachers or heads of department in schools, lecturers in colleges and teachers themselves, to run short courses or school-based workshops.

The handbook is divided into three units. Unit I provides background information leading participants to an appreciation of why the shortfall of girls in science and technology is a cause for professional concern. Unit II explores some of the stereotyped attitudes, of both teachers and pupils, which constitute a barrier to change. Unit III discusses interventions and good practice ideas which teachers can carry out for themselves in school.

Ideally the handbook is intended for use in the context of school-based in-service education, but the units could also form part of a course based in a college or teachers' centre.

There has been increasing concern recently about the underachievement of schoolgirls, especially in mixed schools, and particularly in traditionally 'masculine' areas of the curriculum such as physical sciences, mathematics and technical craft subjects. At various places in the handbook reference is made to the GIST project. GIST (Girls into Science and Technology) was a four-year innovative action research programme which aimed to encourage schoolgirls to opt for science and technology and to consider scientific and technical occupations. The project team worked with teachers in ten co-educational comprehensives in Greater Manchester and with 2000 children who entered secondary school in September 1980. It was financed by the EOC/SSRC Joint Panel, the Schools Council, Department of Industry, Manchester Polytechnic and Shell UK Ltd.

Many of the 'lecturettes' (see note opposite) refer to research evidence from GIST or other sources on sex differences in science and technology. Users of the handbook should follow up these references and extend their presentations by using the references and list of further reading at the end of the handbook.

Teachers in the GIST action schools worked with the project team towards modifying the sex-typing of subjects which appears to be particularly strong in the first three to four years of secondary school. Efforts of various kinds were made to improve girls' attitudes to physical science and to encourage more girls to pursue their scientific studies in the fourth year.

Some of the interventions developed in GIST schools are mentioned here as possible activities for teachers.

Details of the GIST action programme and the outcomes of the project are available in four main publications, listed at the end of this introduction.

*

### How can teachers be made aware of the influence of sex stereotypes on girls' performance in science and technology?

The GIST teacher workshops consisted of three elements: (i) informational, (ii) attitudinal, and (iii) practical, corresponding to the three units in this handbook.

#### (i)    Informational

Teachers study patterns of sex differentiation at school and critically evaluate the extent to which sex-differentiated performance and behaviour at school is biologically or culturally determined.

The shortfall of schoolgirls in science and technology is already a well-recognized problem. Current trends indicate a gradual increase in the numbers of pupils generally taking physical science, and a much slower increase in girls and boys taking craft subjects non-traditional for their sex. However, the rate of change is disappointingly slow. Teachers need to know (or find out) the pattern of sex differences in subject take-up both nationally and in their own school or local authority. A certain amount of information about the possible causes of the apparent avoidance by girls of science and technology is included in this section, together with a summary of the arguments in favour of change.

#### (ii)   Attitudinal

'De-stereotyping' exercises sensitize teachers to sex-role stereotyping as a phenomenon with significant effects for pupils' academic performance as well as for their personal, social and career development. This entails consideration of teachers' own personal views and attitudes. Teachers as professionals are interested in, and willing to accept evidence on, the causes of girls' avoidance of physical science subjects. But unspoken personal attitudes about sex difference often create a barrier to genuine change. Directly confronting or challenging teachers' personal beliefs and attitudes can alienate individuals' willingness to consider the issue seriously and rationally. So the exercises which have been developed here are designed as a non-threatening introduction to 'de-stereotyping'. Directly critical or threatening elements are avoided while allowing teachers to reflect privately on their own views and how these may come to be significant in the classroom. Throughout, the emphasis is on the teachers' professional commitment to providing equal opportunities, although their personal and individual beliefs are also bound to have an impact on the teachers' expectations and interactions with male and female pupils.

#### (iii)  Practical

A third section on practical intervention strategies to be applied in schools and classrooms is based largely on the work of GIST schools in collaboration with the GIST team. For this reason the suggestions are eminently practicable, but should not be regarded as comprehensive. Teachers may well begin to develop their own strategies for change at this stage.

The workshop approach helps teachers devise and apply practical intervention strategies and teaching approaches to reduce sex-related disadvantage.

GIST publications

Catton, John. *Ways and Means: the Craft, Design and Technology Education of Girls* (Schools Council Programme Pamphlets). Longman, York, 1985.

Kelly, A., Whyte, J. and Smail, B. *Girls into Science and Technology: the Final Report*. GIST, 1984, mimeo. (Available from Department of Sociology, University of Manchester, price £1.)

Smail, Barbara. *Girl-friendly Science: Avoiding Sex Bias in the Curriculum* (Schools Council Programme Pamphlets). Longman, York, 1985.

Whyte, Judith. *Girls into Science and Technology: the Story of a Project*. Routledge & Kegan Paul, 1986.

## I.  BACKGROUND INFORMATION

In Unit 1 there are three 'lecturettes' providing materials with further references to help tutors or group leaders present and introduce the following three topics:

1.  What is the girls and science/technology problem?  (20 mins)
2.  Why does it matter?  (10 mins (first part)  15 mins (second part))
3.  What teacher attitudes can help or hinder positive change?  (10 mins)

Lecturette 1 includes two tables and a diagram for use on overhead projectors.  Tables 1 and 2, indicating sex differences in examination entries and take-up of secondary-school subjects, are examples which should be updated by tutors, using the same format.

There are also four workshop activities which can be carried out in school with a group of teachers:

1.  involves the collection of local data linked to the information in Lecturette 1 and Tables 1 and 2 (depending on availability of information:  2-4 hours)

2.  is a quiz about various aspects of women's position in the UK.  The correct answers appear in an appendix (page 64).  (10 mins)

3.  suggests a framework for discussion on girls and science and technology:  why does it matter?  (10 mins)

4.  offers two comments by science teachers which can be used to provoke discussion of the girls and science problem  (20 mins)

The lecturettes and workshop activities appear in the order in which it is suggested tutors/group leaders use them, e.g. Workshop activities 1 and 2 should take place after the presentation of the first part of Lecturette 2.

### Lecturette 1

### What is the girls and science/technology problem?

Is it really true to say that girls are discriminated against in the British school system?

Do schoolgirls 'underachieve' in terms of their potential for success?

The trouble with answering these questions is that the pattern of sex differences in achievement throughout the school years is quite complex, and contains some paradoxes.

Girls, for example, have an intellectual headstart on boys from the earliest years. They say both their first word and their first sentence before boys, and at the age of 2, have larger vocabularies. They count sooner, too. (Coltheart, 1975).

From the beginning of school, girls are on average better than boys not only at reading but in number ability. Their scores on achievement tests are higher and they retain a slight overall lead on boys until the end of junior school (Douglas, 1964; Douglas and Cherry, 1977). Indeed this is why the results of the 11 plus had to be 'rigged' in the past, as girls would otherwise have obtained a 'disproportionate' share (i.e. more than 50 per cent) of grammar-school places. (*New Society*, 12 March 1977).

Girls excel in certain aspects of school work, for example, writing. But 'creative writing' is perceived as a lower-status skill than problem solving or creating your own computer programs. The trouble is that teachers too often assume if girls are good at writing, they are therefore not 'suited' to other kinds of learning such as mathematics, physics or technical crafts.

In the last two or three years, girls have begun to overtake boys in the number of O-level passes they gain. If present trends continue they will soon be getting as many A-level passes, on average, as boys.

Table 1     Summer examinations, 1981

|  | CSE entries | | O-level entries | | A-level entries | |
|---|---|---|---|---|---|---|
|  | boys % | girls % | boys % | girls % | boys % | girls % |
| Mathematics | 48 | 52 | 53 | 47 | 73 | 37 |
| Physics | 82 | 18 | 75 | 25 | 81 | 19 |
| Chemistry | 60 | 40 | 61 | 39 | 67 | 33 |
| Computer studies/science | – | – | 69 | 31 | 77 | 23 |
| Tech.drawing | 96 | 4 | 96 | 4 | 98 | 2 |
| Domestic science/ cookery | 9 | 91 | 3 | 97 | 0.4 | 99.5 |

Source: *Statistics of School Leavers: CSE and GCE (England), 1981* (DES, 1982), tables C25(a) and (b), C28(a) and (b), C29(a) and (b)

So why should there be any complaint about girls' underachievement? At least in primary school, boys appear to be doing less well than they should. And it is they who tend to have more problems with reading and language work.

A closer look at the statistics is necessary. Not until recently has the remarkably clear pattern of sex differences - especially startling in the secondary years - received any detailed attention.

10

The fact is, that despite a commitment to equal opportunity in education for both sexes which has existed in this country since the 1944 Education Act, male and female pupils receive two different and distinct educational packages.

Girls and boys leave school with very different qualifications and prospects. Many girls do not take the sorts of school subjects which lead on to good jobs or apprenticeships or which offer entrance to the majority of courses in further education colleges, polytechnics or universities. In particular, they disqualify themselves from many opportunities by dropping science and technical subjects. Seventy-six per cent of girls leave school with one science pass or none at all. Even since the introduction of 'craft circuses' in secondary schools, 98 per cent of girls turn away from technical crafts.

Table 1 is based simply on the DES statistics of school-leavers published each year. It shows some of the characteristic sex difference patterns in several subjects. For example the ratio of boys to girls entering for O-level physics is 3 : 1 and for A level, 4 : 1. In chemistry the imbalance is not quite so great, with 3 boys for every 2 girls entering at O level, 2 : 1 at A level.

Table 2    O-level entries, summer 1982 (England only)

|  | | % F | % M |
|---|---|---|---|
| 'Feminine' | Needlework | 99.8 | 0.2 |
| | Cookery | 96.6 | 0.3 |
| | Other domestic subjects | 94 | 5.9 |
| | Religious studies | 61.5 | 38.4 |
| | Biology | 64.4 | 35.6 |
| | French | 60 | 39.9 |
| | English literature | 58.2 | 41.7 |
| | English language | 54.2 | 45.7 |
| 'Masculine' | Mathematics | 46.6 | 53.3 |
| | Chemistry | 40.2 | 59.7 |
| | Physics | 26.7 | 73.2 |
| | Technical drawing | 5.2 | 94.7 |
| | Woodwork | 1.6 | 98.3 |
| | Metalwork | 0.44 | 99.5 |

Source: *Statistics of School Leavers: CSE and GCE (England), 1982* (DES, 1983), table C28

Science teachers in particular appreciate clear objective data such as this, as an introduction to the 'girls and science' problem. For craft teachers, the imbalance in 'crossover' of boys or girls to non-traditional subjects can be pointed out, e.g. 9 per cent of CSE entries in domestic science/cookery are from boys, but the largest percentage of girls taking a traditional 'boys' craft' is 4 per cent.

To complete the picture, it can also be helpful to draw up a 'gender spectrum' of subjects, placing those in which more than 50 per cent of entries are from girls at the 'feminine' end of the spectrum, vice versa for the boys. Table 2 is based on O-level entries for 1982 and shows that mathematics, the physical sciences and the technical crafts are all clearly 'masculine' in this sense.

Workshop activity 1

Girls' and boys' choices

1.  Teachers collect information about examination entries for these subjects in their own school and compare the percentages of boys and girls in each subject with the national figures.

2.  Information can also be collected about the most recent option choices for fourth-year subjects.

Lecturette 2

Why does it matter?

Why should there be concern that girls are not gaining the skills, experience and qualifications which can be acquired from school studies of science and technology?

There are three main arguments for change: first, it is part of national educational policy that girls should achieve genuine equality of opportunity in these areas (see 'Educational policy' below). Secondly, there is the argument that female exclusion from science and technology underlies and reinforces female inequality at work. This lecturette lays out the factual bases of this argument in some detail. Thirdly, many science teachers consider that their subjects are an essential element of education for citizenship and that the absence of girls from the physical sciences is an issue of serious professional concern (see Workshop activity 2, p.14).

Educational policy*

Several documents testify to national concern about the shortfall of girls in science and technology:

1.  The educational provisions of the Sex Discrimination Act (1975) require schools to offer the same curriculum to both sexes. In the main, this has been interpreted by schools to mean that

home economics and craft, design and technology should be on offer
to both sexes, at least during the first year of secondary schooling.
However progress in take-up of physics and CDT by girls has been
extremely slow.

2.  The DES publication *The School Curriculum* (DES, 1981a) makes several
    statements concerning equal opportunities:

    'The equal treatment of men and women embodied in our law needs
    to be supported in the curriculum ...'

    'It is essential to ensure that equal opportunities are genuinely
    available to both boys and girls.'

    The document recommends a balanced science curriculum up to the age
    of 16 in order to avoid pupils closing career avenues by making
    inappropriate option choices.

3.  The HMI survey *Girls and Science* (DES, 1981b) offers many
    recommendations for good practice in encouraging girls to participate
    in the physical sciences.  It found that the important features of
    schools which were more than usually successful in encouraging girls
    (and boys) to take physics and chemistry were:  the content of the
    science curriculum, and ways in which subjects were organized and
    taught and particularly the careers guidance programme.  The report
    concluded that 'science for all, to include physical science, should
    be the ultimate goal.'

4.  The consultative document *Science Education in Schools* (DES, 1982)
    states 'Throughout the period of compulsory secondary education
    every school, with the support of its LEA, should adopt the policy
    of giving all pupils a broad science programme which ... gives
    genuinely equal curricular opportunities in science to boys and
    girls.'

5.  Circular 3/84 which outlines procedures and criteria for the
    approval of teacher training courses states that 'Students should
    be prepared ... to teach the full range of pupils with their
    diversity of ability, behaviour, social background and ethnic
    origins.  They will need to learn how to respond flexibly to such
    diversity and to guard against preconceptions based on the race or
    sex of pupils.'  (DES/Welsh Office, 1984)

6.  The criteria for funding TVEI (Technical and Vocational Education
    Initiatives) include the statement that schemes should as far as
    possible avoid sex-stereotyping and that young people of both sexes
    should be educated together.

    The consultative document on CPVE (Certificate of Pre-Vocational
    Education) includes amongst the declared aims of the new 17+
    qualification that CPVE is to 'promote equality of opportunity.'

    YTS schemes have so far offered limited opportunities to young
    women, but the Manpower Services Commission has produced training

---

* Many of these points appear in P. Orr, 'Sex differentiation in schools:
the current situation', in Whyte et al. (eds) (1985).

materials for YTS staff designed to help them understand and combat sex-stereotyping.

7.  In a speech to the Girls' Schools Association (in November 1983), the Secretary of State for Education said that 'Girls' education must reflect the fact that most women will be working for much of their lives; and that many may be the sole or principal breadwinner for a family', and at the North of England Education Conference in Sheffield, January 1984, he advocated a nationally agreed framework for the 5-16 curriculum and nationally agreed objectives for its various components. All pupils should have a curriculum that is broad, balanced, relevant and suitably differentiated to take account of different aptitudes and abilities.

8.  The Association for Science Education (ASE) is committed to the aim of encouraging all pupils, but particularly girls, to continue their study of the physical sciences. (See 'Useful addresses', page 68.)

(Lecturette 2 continues, after Workshop activity 3, on page 17.)

Workshop activity 2

Discussion:  Girls and science and technology:  why does it matter?

Notes

Having established the extent of girls' under-representation in science and technology, groups may then go on to discuss why the issue is to be regarded as a 'problem'.

A useful way to introduce this discussion is to ask teachers to jot down some reasons why they think we should be concerned that girls are not participating fully in these aspects of schooling.

A similar exercise with Manchester teachers produced the following main reasons for concern:

(1)  Science is an important component of education for all pupils, including girls.

(2)  In a technological society all citizens should have sufficient knowledge and understanding of science and technology to contribute to intelligent decision-making about a range of issues such as fluoridization, nuclear power, nutrition, etc.

(3)  The exclusion of women from science and technology limits their opportunities for development.

(4)  The entry of women to science and technology may bring about fruitful changes in scientific and technological practice.

Underlying the gender split in school subjects are expectations about the work men and women will do after school. Lecturette 2, 'Why does it matter?', gives some general information about the sexual division of labour, and the implications for the work of women.

As an introduction to this lecturette, teachers can 'guesstimate' the answers to the following quiz (for answers see Appendix, page 64).

## Quiz

1.  What is the average completed family size in Britain today (i.e. number of children)?

    ☐ 1.76
    ☐ 2.2
    ☐ 2.5

2.  What percentage of British households are made up of working husband, economically inactive wife and two dependent children?

    ☐ 5%
    ☐ 10%
    ☐ 25%

3.  What is the average time taken out of employment by women to form a family?

    ☐ 5 years
    ☐ 7 years
    ☐ 12 years

4.  What % of mothers of children aged 0-4 years are at work (F/T or P/T)?

    ☐ 10%
    ☐ 25%
    ☐ 30%

5.  How many women workers in the UK in 1979?

    ☐ 3 million
    ☐ 10 million
    ☐ 20 million

6.  What % of the labour force is female?

    ☐ 29%
    ☐ 40%
    ☐ 50%

7.  What % of headteachers of secondary schools were women in 1975?

    ☐ 20%
    ☐ 30%
    ☐ 40%

8.  What % of pupils entering for O-level physics in 1981 were girls?

    ☐ 26%
    ☐ 30%
    ☐ 38%

9.  What % of pupils entering for O-level cookery in 1981 were boys?

    ☐ 0.2%
    ☐ 3%
    ☐ 16%

10. Most women come back into the labour market after their youngest child starts school. How many years between then and retirement age?

    ☐ 10 years
    ☐ 18 years
    ☐ 25 years

Lecturette 2 (contd)

## Why does it matter?

### The work of women

Forty per cent of the British labour force is female:  about nine million
women, compared with just under fifteen million men are employed outside
the home.  However the labour market is quite rigidly divided by sex.
Almost two million women work in occupations where over 90 per cent of
the employees are female:  typists, secretaries, maids, nurses, canteen
assistants, sewing machinists.  Women also form the majority of cooks,
kitchen staff, bar staff, office cleaners, hairdressers, launderers,
clothing makers, waiting staff and housekeepers.  Women work in spheres
of the labour market which can be seen as an extension of the
traditional female domestic role.  Or, in the language of labour
economics, women's jobs are in the 'secondary' or service sector
containing lower paid and relatively insecure jobs.  The problem of
excessively low pay is largely a problem for women workers.

The reasons why women are clustered in the lower paid and less
secure sectors of employment are twofold:  they do not have the right
qualifications to get the better paid more stable jobs, and secondly
they are expected to bear an added burden of domestic responsibilities
for childcare and housework.  The increase in the proportion of married
women working has not been matched by changes in men's participation in
unpaid work at home.  The two reasons for women's disadvantaged
position in the labour market are connected.  Generally speaking women,
or rather girls, do not try to obtain the 'right' qualifications because
of the expectation that in their adult lives they will engage in 'women's
work'.

Occupations are also sex segregated in another way.  Where men and
women work in the same industry or sector, men typically work at higher
grades:  non-manual rather than manual, skilled rather than unskilled:
most management and leadership positions are held by men.

Both 'horizontal' segregation (certain occupations regarded as
typically masculine or feminine) and 'vertical' segregation (men in
senior, women in subordinate positions) are reinforced by the channelling
of children into different subject areas at school, and the assumption
about adult responsibilities which children acquire during the school
years.

Why should a change in the patterns of occupational sex segregation
be considered desirable?

The most basic argument is one of justice and equality.  As women
are making as substantial a social contribution by their work as men,
it is unjust that they should continue to receive so much less pay and
that their opportunities for advancement and self-realization should be
artificially limited by the traditional division into 'men's' and
'women's' work.

The chief stumbling block to acceptance of this argument lies in
traditionalist beliefs about women's role as being essentially at the
service of men and children.  But a case for change can be based on the

17

shifts which have already occurred in women's life patterns. Figure 1 graphically presents the dramatic change in women's role in the last century.

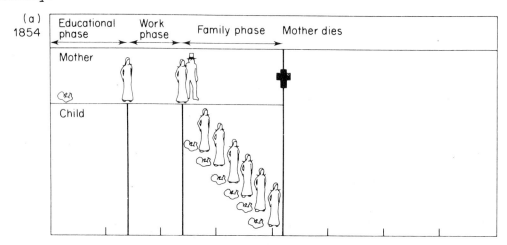

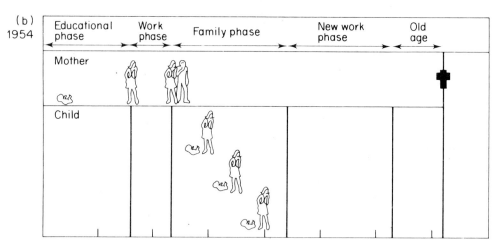

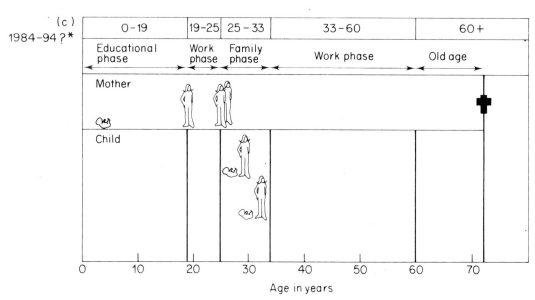

Age in years

*   Based on current statistical trends, 1982.

Figure 1   Development of women's two-phase working life.
Adapted from a diagram by Ann Oakley, in 'The myth of motherhood',
*New Society*, 26 February 1970, p. 351.   Source:   A. Myrdal and
V. Klein, *Women's Two Roles* (Routledge & Kegan Paul, 1956);   Office
of Population Censuses and Surveys, *General Household Survey*, *1976*
(HMSO, 1978), table 4.5;   and Equal Opportunities Commission, 'The
Fact about Women is ...' (fact card), 1982.

The major change in Britain is the profile of the typical working woman. In 1901 she was likely to be young (13-24) and single. In 1984, the 'economical activity rate' (employment outside the home) is higher for women aged 45-54 than the rate for young women. This is the complete opposite of the pattern at the start of the century.

## Women's changing life patterns

These notes refer directly to Figure 1.

### Children

In 1854 the average woman had six children and was dead by the age of 50. Of course, as this is an average, it means that many women had considerably more than six children, while some (probably middle-aged and upper-class women) had fewer than six. Some women died in their twenties while others might live on to enjoy old age.

A century later, the average family size had reduced to three. While the mother in 1854 spent fifteen years of her life pregnant or breastfeeding, the woman of 1954 needed to spend only four years in that state.

The availability of reliable contraception allowed women to plan their families and the average woman had three children spaced closely together.

In 1984 the average completed family size is down to 1.7. As this is an average it means of course that many couples are remaining childless or having only one child.

Life expectancy for women is now higher than that for men. The average woman can expect to live until she is 76, the average man until he is 69.9.

### Education

Since the 1850s the average school-leaving age has progressively risen. With current training initiatives for school-leavers, the effective completion of the educational phase is now at 19. This accentuates the trend for the typical working women to be in an older age group.

### Employment

In the 1850s women left employment when they married; in the 1950s most women continued working until they had their first child. In the 1980s, increasing numbers of women are absent from paid employment for a relatively short time - an average of from 5 to 7 years. Quite a number will go back to part-time work between the births of their children, while a smaller proportion take only the statutory maternity leave. Most return to work part or full time when the younger child starts school when they are aged 33 to 35. They have approximately 25 years of employment ahead of them, if they retire at 60. In 1976, 72 per cent of women aged 35 to 49 were working full time or part time.

Fifteen years from now, many of today's schoolgirl leavers will be re-entrants to the labour market with a prospect of 25 years of employment, compared with 30 years for their male contemporaries.

But many of the traditional feminine occupations will have disappeared, for example, typing or supermarket check-out jobs. For many women the option of staying at home is unavailable or entails poverty. In 1976 23 per cent of heads of household were female, and some 11 per cent of all families with dependent children were one-parent families, the majority with a female 'breadwinner', compared with 8 per cent in 1971. The increases in breakdown of marriage and the incidence of lone or unmarried mothers shows no sign of abating (OPCS, 1978). The only remaining alternative for women is desegregation of the labour market and access for females to formerly male employment areas.

These patterns indicate the need for women to gain qualifications, especially in science and technology, which will fit them for entry to related occupations.

Lecturette 3

What teacher attitudes can help or hinder positive change?

Recent research has shown that conservative teacher views, for instance about married women who work or the value of technology, are a major stumbling block to equal educational opportunities for girls. A national survey found a large minority of teachers opposed to or doubtful about equal opportunity practices though not the broad policies. Men were more likely to be negative but subject taught, rather than sex, distinguished those who favoured and those who were against equal opportunities. Teachers of mathematics, physical sciences, technical crafts subjects, mostly men, were most negative. (Pratt et al., 1984)

In an interesting small-scale study, science teachers were asked to rate third-year pupils' science scripts, and to estimate suitability for O-level entrance. When the teachers thought the script was by a girl their rating of scientific grasp and potential for O level was significantly lower than when they believed the work was by a boy, although the scripts were identical. (Spear, 1984)

Teachers involved on the GIST project claimed to be practising equal opportunities already, and said they had made few changes as a result of GIST. However evaluation showed that many teachers had reviewed curriculum materials or approaches, become more conscious of the impact of stereotyped language, or altered their teaching methods and classroom management as a result of observation with feedback.

For example some teachers dispensed with the system of addressing general questions to the class, which usually results in mostly boys putting up their hands to answer, and instead directed questions to specific individuals. These teachers claimed that they had always encouraged girls to participate in class, and seem to have incorporated the new strategies into their own thinking. The evaluators suggested that they were perhaps unwilling to admit to possible bias in the past. Other teachers expressed doubt about actually saying to children that women could become scientists, on the grounds that such positive encouragement might be regarded as propaganda. Teachers without these worries, notably in schools with a more progressive atmosphere, openly discussed the issue with pupils. Changes in pupil attitudes and subject choices (for both boys and girls) were greatest in schools where teachers were most open with their pupils. (See Payne et al. (1984), Kelly, Whyte and Smail (1984).)

The implication is that positive teacher attitudes can be an important influence on girls who are hesitating about the choice of science or crafts subjects in the fourth year. However the positive encouragement needs to be fairly explicit if it is to result in greater participation by girls.


Workshop activity 4

Discussion of science teachers' views

For discussion

These two extracts are from letters sent to Alison Kelly and published in *The Missing Half: Girls and Science Education* (1981). What do you think of them?

'I think that the problem is in many ways historical and is paralleled in many other male-dominated professions. Physical scientists have, for many years, been almost exclusively men, or perhaps more correctly the ones to achieve eminence have been. Either consciously or unconsciously, this has influenced the teaching method to maintain the status quo. Most physical science textbooks and courses are designed to appeal to what are socially acceptable masculine interests - mechanical things, industrial technology, explosives, etc. Yet logically there is no valid reason why this should be so. For example, I think that one of the best methods of teaching the mechanisms of heat transfer is to relate them to cooking.

What I am really saying is that the problem is of our own creation. We do not offer in schools physical science courses which are suitable for both boys and girls, instead we offer courses designed for boys, which the girls can take if they wish or dare.'

(Male physical science teacher, mixed secondary modern school)


'It is a fact that most girls have not the type of mind that faces a problem nor reasons well from given data - not even my star girls, who got as far as Oxford and/or Cambridge, and to a first and a PhD in one case. Even this girl just could not compare with her boy rivals but she took the subject further and at a university where standards were lower.'

(Male physics teacher, mixed grammar school)

## II.  ATTITUDES

The second part of this handbook addresses teacher attitudes which may discourage girls from science and technology.

Unit II has six lecturettes providing material with further references to help tutors or group leaders present and introduce the following topics:

4  Why don't girls do science?  the biological evidence (15 mins)

5  Why don't girls do science?  the evidence from socialization (15 mins)

6  What are gender stereotypes?  (10 mins)

7  Gender bias in learning resources  (10 mins)

8  Classroom interactions  (10 mins)

9  Subject options  (20 mins)

Table 3 illustrates sex differences in girls' and boys' experience of constructional activities and can be used as an overhead projector transparency linked with Lecturette 5.

Explanations of sex differences in achievement may emphasize biological or socialization factors.  Lecturettes 4 and 5 set out some of the main arguments.

There are five workshop activities which can be carried out in school with a group of teachers:

5  'Brainstorming' is a short group exercise exploring cultural stereotypes about sex roles  (15 mins)

6  'Denis/Denise' is a group discussion simulating teacher responses to pupils according to gender  (35 mins)

7  is an exercise using a sentence completion questionnaire to provoke discussion on teachers' stereotyped responses to colleagues and pupils  (15 mins)

8  involves the examination of learning resources for gender bias (1-2 hours depending on resources used)

9  offers five points for discussion concerning the arrangements for subject options in participants' schools  (30 mins-1 hour)

Teachers are generally interested in the facts and statistics which demonstrate that girls are under-represented in science and technology, but simply providing information is not sufficient to convince them that anything could or should be done about it.  The 'de-stereotyping' exercises (Workshop activities 5, 6 and 7) highlight common assumptions about the two sexes which may indirectly affect classroom interaction and participation.

Numerous studies have shown that textbooks and resources are biased towards boys' interests; rather than quote these sources it is more effective to ask teachers to examine books and materials themselves. They are generally surprised by the bias which it is only too easy to find. Lecturette 7 and Workshop activity 8 introduce this work.

Teachers can, usually unintentionally, reinforce stereotyping of school subjects by their assumptions about pupils' abilities and interests, leading them to treat boys and girls differently. Research indicates that boys succeed in 'dominating' the mixed classroom. This may in part be because of the more boisterous behaviour of boys and the consequent need to keep them in check and maintain their interest. Unfortunately it can have the unintended effect that girls' needs and interests seem to be disregarded. Lecturette 8 discusses classroom interactions.

The majority of teachers believe themselves to be genuinely committed to equal opportunities, and it is therefore important to stress the professional implications of unintended sex differentiation. Lecturette 9 discusses how subject option processes 'channel' girls out of science and technology.

If teachers become professionally interested in the question of girls' avoidance of science and technology, they are more willing to consider developing and applying appropriate intervention strategies, covered in the third part of this handbook.


Lecturette 4

Why don't girls do science? the biological evidence

Do boys and girls differ in their innate abilities or is it just a question of differing interests? Initially at least, girls seem more interested in biology and less interested in physics and chemistry. Do girls 'drop out' of science as it gets harder, because they have less science ability than boys or because they lack the motivation to succeed? Do boys and girls differ in learning style? Are modern teaching methods more suited to the boys' way of learning? Does the masculine image of science and technology seem to exclude girls?

Every science teacher will have his or her own theories and opinions about these questions, but teachers of science and mathematics may be particularly prone to accept explanations of girls' avoidance of science as lying in some deficiency of girls rather than in the way the subject is presented in the school context. Research into this question suggests that there is a small but measurable difference between the performance of girls and boys on standardized science tests even at the age of 10 years. So the factors which cause girls to avoid physical sciences begin to operate in the early years before any formal science education has started. Possible explanations of this initial sex difference can be divided into two groups, with a focus on biological or socialization differences:

<u>Biological evidence</u>   Most biological theories concentrate on the sex difference which has been observed in spatial ability (the ability to visualize objects in three dimensions and to perceive relationships in spatial orientation).  On average, males do better than females on tests of spatial ability and some studies suggest that physical scientists perform better than arts, social science or biological science specialists in these tests.  However, the gap between the sexes in spatial ability is considerably smaller than the gap between the sexes in science achievement.  Therefore the difference in spatial ability can be, at most, a partial explanation.

Possible biological reasons for the sex difference in spatial ability are still being discussed.  The theories proposed link spatial ability to genetic factors, hormone levels or brain lateralization.

The genetic theory suggests that spatial ability is partially determined by a recessive X-linked gene which is present in 50 per cent of males and 25 per cent of females.  This theory has formed the basis of several studies which have invest-igated the pattern of spatial ability within families.  The more recent studies do not provide any concrete evidence to support the theory.

The hormonal theory suggests that, since males and females have differing levels of androgen and oestrogen, the sex difference in spatial ability could be explained in terms of hormone effects on the nervous system.  The evidence to support or disprove this theory in humans is not available at the present time.

Another theory, open to much speculation, is that of brain lateralization.  One side of the brain is known to control verbal skills, the other side to control spatial skills. Girls, as part of their earlier maturation, become more pro-ficient than boys in verbal skills.  They may then come to rely on these skills in problem-solving situations and do not develop their spatial skills to compensate.  Much more work is needed into this field before definite conclusions can be reached.

    For teachers, the <u>practical</u> implications are minimal.  We know that biological factors cannot account satisfactorily for <u>all</u> the observed sex differences, and that social conditioning, in the widest sense, is also of tremendous importance.

    Some recent research suggests that when boys' and girls' different experiences and choice of subjects is taken into account, the remaining gap between the sexes is very small indeed.  For example, in the United States, where more girls tend to drop mathematics, it was sometimes assumed that the explanation lay in a sex difference in spatial ability. But the girls who dropped mathematics were also less likely to take other courses which had a component of spatial learning.  When differences between boys and girls in the number of 'space-related' courses they had taken were allowed for, the sex-related differences in spatial visualiza-tion were largely eliminated (Fennema and Sherman, 1977).

Table 3   Sex differences in constructional activities

|  | % saying they do this 'quite often' | |
| --- | --- | --- |
|  | Girls | Boys |
| Build models (like Airfix kits) | 12 | 59 |
| Play with a construction kit (like Lego or Meccano) | 28 | 48 |
| Make paper aeroplanes | 22 | 48 |

Source:  Kelly, Smail and Whyte (1981)

A comparable study of girls and boys who had taken O-level mathematics in England and Wales showed that when mathematics-related elements in other subjects such as physics or technical drawing were taken into account, no difference could be found in boys' and girls' performance. (Sharma and Meighan, 1980)

The GIST project explored whether there were significant differences in girls' and boys' pre-scientific, technical and 'tinkering' experiences acquired informally outside school.  In fact boys were considerably more likely than girls to have experience in using tools such as a saw or a screwdriver, helping to maintain a car or bicycle and playing with constructional and electrical toys. (See Table 3.)

This has obvious implications for performance in science and crafts subjects.  If tools and apparatus are unfamiliar to girls they may be hesitant about using them.  If they have not played with constructional and electrical toys they will not have picked up the rudiments of mechanics and circuitry to the same extent as boys.


Lecturette 5

Why don't girls do science?  the evidence from socialization

Socialization is the cultural process of passing on patterns of behaviour, attitudes and beliefs to the next generation.  Expectations about boys and girls, men and women, are an important element of socialization and are reinforced primarily by parents, teachers, peer group and the media.

*Socialization at home*

Girls and boys learn to adopt different behaviour and attitudes in line with what is considered 'appropriate' for each sex.  Certain types of behaviour are reinforced by reward and punishment.  For instance, a large study of child-rearing found the most consistent difference in parents' treatment was to to discourage any sign of aggression in girls, while allowing boys to be more aggressive and 'fight back' if another child started a quarrel.  (Sears, Maccoby and Levin, 1957)

Boys are more likely to be bought toys such as mechanical building kits, electric trains and chemistry sets, which help them to develop scientific skills. Gifts typically given to girls, dolls, imitation housework toys, clothes or jewellery, encourage them to be aware of the needs of others and conscious of their own appearance. A survey by Acorn Computers found that boys were thirteen times more likely to be bought a home computer than girls.

These different experiences predispose boys and girls to differential interests in topics and subjects taught at school. Eleven-year-old children in GIST schools had approximately equal scores on a science knowledge test, but their curiosity about scientific topics was clearly divided along sex lines. Boys were more interested in physical science, girls in biology and nature study. Unfortunately, science teaching tends too often to build on boys' rather than girls' existing interests, reinforcing the idea that science is for boys, and so widening the gap between the sexes.

Boys seem to be under more pressure to 'act like boys'; they get stronger negative reactions from parents for 'effeminate' behaviour than girls do for being 'tomboyish'. This may be why boys tend to have more rigid attitudes about sex roles than girls. In the GIST survey girls, but not boys, thought that boys should 'help with the housework', 'make the beds' and 'learn to sew'. In general boys disapproved of girls engaging in 'masculine' activities such as 'having an adventure', 'climbing trees' or 'playing football', while girls were more likely to see these as suitable for girls as well as boys.

Boys' attitudes may have crucial effects on girls' behaviour and choices in the mixed school. For example, girls tend to see both sexes as being equally good at 'doing scientific experiments' or 'being a leader', but boys claim to be better at these. A substantial proportion of GIST girls saw woodwork as a male subject, but it was even more strongly sex-typed by boys: 79 per cent of them but only 47 per cent of girls thought the boys were better at woodwork.

These attitude findings indicate that with children of this age (11-12) one needs to keep in mind that the two sexes already feel themselves to belong to two distinct groups, and are perhaps over conscious of differences of behaviour. As they get older, they become a little more liberal about sex roles, but the gap between boys and girls stays the same, pinpointing the need to address the stereotypes held by boy pupils especially.

See Workshop activity 5, 'Brainstorming' and Lecturette 6, 'What are gender stereotypes?' (page 31).

Workshop activity 5

Brainstorming

Goals:          1.  To clarify the concept of a sex-role 'stereotype'

                2.  A 'warm-up' exercise to precede 'Denis/Denise'

Group size:     Small groups of 6-10

Time required:  Approximately 15 minutes

Materials:       Paper and pens

Process:         1.  Group members are asked to 'brainstorm' and
                     generate a list of adjectives which society
                     applies or which they believe apply to women.

                 2.  Same exercise repeated, only groups are to
                     produce a list of adjectives applying to men.

                 3.  Lists are compared and common themes discussed.

Variations:      1.  Instead of 'women' and 'men' adjectives can be
                     those applied to 'women teachers' or 'boys at
                     school'

                 2.  Groups can consider which adjectives are
                     parallel and opposite for the two sexes, e.g.
                     aggressive-passive; sensitive-blunt, and/or
                     whether there are more or fewer negative
                     adjectives for men/women.


Notes

As societal and personal values are deliberately confused, this
exercise is almost completely 'non-threatening'.  Used with mixed
groups of practising teachers it usually provokes laughter and
group interaction.  However it does also clarify the nature of sex-
role stereotyping in our culture while encouraging private consideration of participants' own stereotypical assumptions.


(Adapted by the author from a similar exercise by J. Bould and
B. Hopson, University of Leeds Careers and Counselling Unit - see
their 'In-service training:  raising teachers' awareness of sex role
stereotyping in schools' (University of Leeds, 1980, mimeo).)


Workshop activity 6

Denis/Denise:  gender stimulus game

Goals            1.  To obtain first-hand experience of how the single
                     stimulus of gender may structure responses to pupils.

                 2.  To provoke discussion and awareness of sex-role
                     stereotyping.

Group size:      A minimum of 10 participants divided into two, four or
                 six groups.  Each group should be composed of 5-7
                 members.  Any even number of groups can be accommodated.

Time required: Approximately 35-40 minutes

Materials:       Case study sheets for 'Denis' and 'Denise' (see below).

Physical setting: Separate rooms for 'Denis' and 'Denise' groups or a
                  room large enough to accommodate two sets of small
                  group discussions.  'Denis' and 'Denise' groups should
                  be far enough apart so that they cannot overhear one
                  another's discussions.

Process:    1.  The tutor/group leader introduces the game as a 'group
                consensus exercise', and instructs the groups that they
                are to reach agreement as a group on the answers to the
                two questions which appear at the bottom of the case
                study sheets.

            2.  Groups are asked to appoint a 'rapporteur' who will chair
                the discussion and be responsible for reporting back the
                group's decision.

            3.  Tutor stresses that all groups have the same information.
                No further information is available and decisions must be
                based on the data which have been provided.  Groups have
                precisely 7 minutes to reach agreement.

            4.  Participants engage in group discussion.  As discussion
                proceeds, tutor should stress from time to time the need
                to reach a consensus decision within the time limit.

            5.  Report-back session:  rapporteurs report group decisions
                and explain the reasons for them.

            6.  Participants are likely to realize almost immediately that
                some groups have received a 'Denis', others a 'Denise'
                sheet.  Tutor can now reveal that some groups had a case
                study about 'Denis', others about 'Denise', but that
                otherwise the information provided was identical.

            7.  Discussion can then focus on differences which occurred
                because of the differential gender stimulus, and also on
                the way that the discussants arrived at their group
                decision.

## Variations

1.  More time can be allowed for discussion.

2.  Tutor can require that rapporteurs must be female.
    Further discussion might centre round feelings generated by this
    instruction, e.g. is there sometimes an unspoken assumption that
    group leaders ought to be male?  Is positive discrimination of
    this kind justified?

3.  Groups may be single sex.

## Notes

When this exercise was carried out with practising teachers, the
careers predicted for Denis led to higher status, higher income occupations than those predicted for Denise.  In general the emphasis of
group decisions varied according to the supposed sex of the pupil, for
example

    (a)  A factor of being 'interested in helping people' tended to be
         overvalued for Denise (e.g. predicted to be a hotel reception-
         ist, personnel manager or nurse, all jobs directly dealing
         with people) but undervalued for Denis, frequently suggested
         to be a bank manager or 'in commerce', i.e. less directly
         involved with people.

    (b)  Predictions about Denise at age 30 may make reference to her
         family situation, e.g. 'working part-time because she is

married with two children', while Denis's marital/parental status may not be mentioned at all, or alternatively referred to as a reason for occupational ambition.

(Adapted from the original exercise developed by the Minnesota Resource Centre for Social Work Education, see *Intervention Strategies for Changing Sex Role Stereotypes: a Procedural Guide* by E.T. Nickerson et al. (Kendall Hunt Publishing, Dubuque, Iowa, USA, 1975).)

CASE STUDY

Denis Johnson, aged 16 years has the following characteristics

1. well-liked by staff and pupils;
2. good looking;
3. careful, persevering worker;
4. has four O levels, all with good grades, in English, mathematics, design, geography;
5. interested in 'helping people'
6. ambitious;  but
7. would like to start earning money as soon as possible.

*Group task*

On the basis of the above information, your group is to reach an agreed consensus on

(a) What Denis is likely to be doing one year after leaving school (i.e. decide first at what age you would expect him to have left school).

(b) What Denis is likely to be doing when he is 30 years of age.

CASE STUDY

Denise Johnson, aged 16 years has the following characteristics

1. well-liked by staff and pupils;
2. good looking;
3. careful, persevering worker;
4. has four O levels, all with good grades, in English, mathematics, design, geography;
5. interested in 'helping people'
6. ambitious;  but
7. would like to start earning money as soon as possible.

*Group task*

On the basis of the above information, your group is to reach an agreed consensus on

(a) What Denise is likely to be doing one year after leaving school (i.e. decide first at what age you would expect her to have left school).

(b) What Denise is likely to be doing when she is 30 years of age.

Lecturette 6

## What are gender stereotypes?

A definition of sex-role stereotyping might be:

> a collection of commonly-held beliefs or opinions about
> 'appropriate' male and female behaviour. Behaviour considered
> suitable for men is labelled 'masculine' and for women 'feminine'

The consensus of opinion on these labels is remarkable, e.g. one
study in the US by Broverman (1970) found that 'masculine'
characteristics included:

| | | |
|---|---|---|
| competence | rationality | assertion |
| aggression | dominance | self-confidence |

and that men were expected to be rough, blunt, with little need for
security, little capacity to express tender feelings and little awareness of the feelings of others.

Feminity required warmth and expressiveness; it was 'feminine' to
be gentle, tactful, quiet, aware of the feelings of others. Women were
expected to be submissive, passive, illogical, unskilled in business,
indecisive, unambitious and lacking in confidence.

There is evidence that this consensus of knowledge of sex stereotypes is arrived at through a process of learning very like the
development of children's knowledge of number or geographical knowledge.
For instance, there is regular systematic development and refinement of
sex-role stereotypes between the ages of 5 and 11 (Best et al., 1977).

At age 5 children are aware of only a few of the more salient
stereotype characteristics - that women are supposed to be gentle and
affectionate, and men strong and aggressive. Not until later ages are
fussy/nagging and flirtatious/charming associated with women and
severe/stern and logical/rational with men. These children lived in
North Carolina, USA, Bristol and Dublin. Children from other cultures
might have produced very different stereotypes.

Children's ideas about sex roles are not necessarily related to
their first-hand experience. One researcher spoke to a 4-year-old
girl whose mother was a doctor, but who believed 'only men can be
doctors, women are nurses'.


## Workshop activity 7

### Sentence completion

Goals:      1. To provoke discussion on teachers' stereotyped
              responses to colleagues and pupils at school.

            2. To relate the knowledge gained about sex-role
              stereotypes to concrete situations in school.

Group size:   Any number

Time required:  Approximately 15 minutes

Materials:  Sentence Completion Questionnaire

Process:

1.  Tutor explains that this exercise is concerned with day-to-day school life. Participants should imagine themselves in the familiar setting of their own school and classroom, and try to keep in mind their most recent interactions with colleagues and pupils.

2.  Tutor explains that the 15 sentences on the Sentence Completion Questionnaire are unfinished. Each individual is to work through them, completing each sentence with the first appropriate phrase which comes to mind. They should not think too deeply about their response, and should carry out the task fairly rapidly.

3.  When individuals have completed all the sentences, tutor asks them to compare their own responses to the following pairs of questions:

    1 and 8
    2 and 9
    5 and 11
    6 and 12
    7 and 13
    10 and 4
    14 and 15

4.  Tutor asks if there are any significant differences which suggest different responses to members of one sex or the other. What are the implications for practice in schools?

Notes

1.  To encourage uninhibited responses, it may be stressed that at no stage will the sheets be seen by anyone else. Individuals thus choose whether or not to report patterns of difference in their own replies.

2.  Generally differences of response will be found between the pairs of questions. For example, sometimes people tend to say they would react more sympathetically to a crying boy than a girl, perhaps reflecting the cultural expectation that boys seldom cry.

See Lecturette 3, 'What teacher attitudes can help or hinder positive change?' (page 20).

SENTENCE COMPLETION QUESTIONNAIRE

This is an individual task.

The fifteen sentences below are unfinished. Complete them with the first appropriate phrase which comes into your head. Do not think too deeply about your answers at this stage. Do the task speedily.

1. In school, I get upset when I see a girl

2. I have learned that boys should never

3. As a woman (or man) teacher I would never

4. I respond to crying boys by

5. Our school teaches girls that they should

6. Noisy and disruptive boys in lessons

7. Girls are annoying to me in my lessons when

8. In school, I get upset when I see a boy

9. I have learned that girls should never

10. I respond to crying girls by

11. Our school teaches boys that they should

12. Noisy and disruptive girls in lessons

13. Boys are annoying to me in my lessons, when

14. I admire women staff for their

15. I admire men staff for their


Lecturette 7

School-based factors:  gender bias in learning resources

Children's books, including many science textbooks, often portray boys
in an active role, e.g. climbing a tree or doing an experiment while
the girls in the picture passively watch.  In most science textbooks
boys predominate in the illustrations, and male people in the examples.

Well-known science schemes such as *Nuffield Combined Science*
(Nuffield Chelsea Curriculum Trust, 1970, *Science for the 70s* (Mee et
al., 1971 and 1972) and *Insight to Science* (ILEA, 1979) were analysed
for sex bias by Barbara Smail of the GIST team.  She reports on the
continuing male bias even in revised versions (Smail, 1985).  A
recurring motif is that illustrations and references in the text to
women and girls almost always cast them in domestic, stereotyped roles
rather than as people involved in science.  Textbooks used for craft,
design and technology are even less likely to feature girls.

Even when material or resources are not sex-typed, for example,
when there are few examples of people anyway, problems still remain.
Girls (and boys) appreciate learning about the social applications of
physical science.  This element is often missing from textbooks or
schemes, concentrating more on the knowledge to be acquired.  Sometimes,
in an effort to make the material more interesting to children teachers
will call up examples which unfortunately tend to appeal more to boys.

For example, in a lesson on circuits, the teacher inquired 'has anyone ever smashed a transistor radio, pulled one apart or looked at any electronics?' The question was unintentionally boy-oriented because girls do not often smash things or even pull them apart.*

In another lesson on light eclipses and refractions the teacher chose to use a football to represent the earth, provoking comments amongst the boys about whose it was, why it was confiscated, etc. The use of a netball, a balloon or a globe would have removed the masculine element from the demonstration.*

Resources and teaching approaches which seem automatically geared to boys' existing interests, thereby exclude girls and contribute to a sense that science is not for them.


## Workshop activity 8

### Reviewing educational resources for gender bias

| | |
|---|---|
| Goal: | To allow teachers to discover for themselves the prevalence of gender bias in textbooks and materials. |
| Group size: | Any |
| Time required: | Approximately 30 minutes of private study (possibly between workshops) plus 20 minutes of group discussion. |

Materials:   1. Science textbooks, crafts worksheets or other resources currently used by participants.

2. Gender bias checklist (see below).

Process:   1. Participants are asked to select for study a textbook chapter from a textbook, worksheet or other pupil resource currently in use in their own classrooms.

2. Participants use Gender bias checklist to analyse chosen materials.

3. Report-back session and discussion of findings.

## Gender bias checklist

1. <u>Count</u> the illustrations

How many show girls/women?   ☐

How many show boys/men?   ☐

Indeterminate   ☐

---

* Examples culled from observations in GIST schools.

2.  Is there any difference in the type of things males and females are shown doing?

    List, for example, swimming, looking puzzled, etc.

3.  Analyse the text and examples

    How many times are females mentioned?  ☐

    How many times are males mentioned?  ☐

4.  Are the examples slanted to girls' or boys' interests?

    List, for example, football/cars/dolls, etc.

### Notes

In many science or technology textbooks there may be scarcely any illustrations or references in the text to people at all.  Tutor may point out that this is not evidence of an unbiased approach, as the lack of social-human implications and applications of science means girls are <u>less</u> likely to be interested in the materials.

## Lecturette 8

### School-based factors:  classroom interactions

In a study based in Birmingham comprehensives the authors found that fifth-form girls showed no preference for male or female staff, but made many comments about the differential treatment they received. Teachers were said to be harsher with boys, but to give them more attention, or friendliness, while girls were treated as 'helpless' or stupid (Davies and Meighan, 1975).

Teachers often find it hard to believe that they treat boys and girls differently.  During the GIST project, which was carried out in co-educational comprehensive schools, teachers invited team members to observe interactions in their classroom, using a simple observational schedule.  Naturally teachers made special efforts to get girls fully involved in the lessons, and many achieved a 50/50 interaction rate. However they were all surprised at the effort it took, and many remarked they had felt as if they were ignoring the boys and giving all their attention to the girls.  This indicates the 'normality' of a classroom situation in which girls take a back seat and participate less fully than boys.

Observations also showed how boys subtly, or often not so subtly, let girls know that science and technology are properly boys' subjects. For instance in a CDT lesson a boy wanted a hand-drill which a girl was using.  His method was not to ask her to pass the tool across when she had finished, but rather to place himself alongside her, fold his arms and stare at the tool.  The girl gave in before completing her drilling and was on the point of handing over the tool when the teacher intervened.

Another workshop incident centred on the need for several pupils to use a polisher.  Girls queued quietly, but boys pestered and rushed the girls to finish;  one even used the edge of the polisher while a girl was still working.

A science class dispersed to start practical work on heating carbohydrates.  They were told that, as there were not enough safety glasses for everyone only those actually heating the test tube needed to wear them, and the others should stand well clear.  Boys rushed to collect glasses and other apparatus.  In some groups of four boys, all were wearing glasses.  The girls' groups had no glasses and had to negotiate with the boys, or call on the teacher to help.  In consequence all the boys had started working before any of the girls' groups.  This was a very interesting incident.  It shows how a seemingly trivial event can lead to them appearing to work more quickly and efficiently.  Girls were 'learning to lose' in science as boys asserted their dominance.

Some frogspawn was brought into a biology lesson so the teacher instructed the pupils to come and look when they had finished their work.  Four or five boys (who had not even started their work) immediately crowded round the fish tank and discussed frogspawn at length.  The observer suggested to a girl sitting nearby, that she should go and look too, but she said, 'No, miss, you can't get in.' It was true, the boys left no space for anyone else to see.  This may be why none of the other girls went near the tank until the teacher issued a general invitation to those who had not yet seen the frogspawn to have a closer look.

Even in this biology lesson, supposedly the 'girls' science', the teacher remarked that the girls seemed less interested.  But the girls' apparent unwillingness might simply have been a disinclination to jockey for a place with the boys.  As in the mathematics and the practical science lesson, girls appear to need specific directives before they will participate in class work of a public or semi-public nature.

(Some of the incidents noted by the GIST team during observations have been dramatically reconstructed in a 16-minute video to provide a focus for teacher discussion - see Unit III,'1. Notes on the video *Fair Shares*'.)


Lecturette 9

Subject  options

It is during the crucial third year of secondary school that girls most rapidly lose interest in science and technical subjects.  Enforced subject choice at 13+ almost certainly militates against all but a minority of girls choosing physics or craft, design and technology. In schools where the choice of science subjects is postponed to the sixth form HMI found that more girls continue with physics and more boys continue with biology to A level than in other schools.  This is probably because they can assess their own individual aptitudes and interests more realistically at this age.  Few other countries allow such early specialization as England and Wales.  For example, the

French baccalauréat and the German Abitur both demand that a broad range of subjects be studied right up to university entrance level.  In Sweden an already limited options system is being curtailed still further, precisely because it has been shown to be a channel through which children express their sex stereotyping, and this is felt to be deleterious to their development as human beings.

For the present, most English schools will continue to offer option choices at the end of the third year, with the predictable outcome that girls will opt out of craft, design and technology and the physical sciences.  Both teachers' and pupils' attitudes are weighted against non-traditional choices.  Five problem areas can be distinguished:

1.  the basis for pupil decision-making

2.  the need to choose between subjects

3.  parental influence

4.  option booklets and information

5.  pupils' fear of being the 'odd one out'.

## 1.  The basis on which pupils make decisions

Subject choices are important decisions which require a lot of thought; there is wide variation in the amount of help given to children to develop the skills of decision-making.

Because subject specialization occurs at a relatively early stage in secondary schools, children are often making choices which may be crucial for future occupational choices, but with very little if any, career guidance.

The GIST project followed approximately 2000 children from the age of 11 when they entered secondary school to 13+ when they made their options for the fourth year.  Their attitudes to school and to science were investigated in the GIST initial survey, taken in the first term of the first year (Kelly, Smail and Whyte, 1981).

The second GIST survey (see Kelly, Whyte and Smail, 1984) asked children about the reasons for their subject choices just after they had made them.  For both boys and girls the most important factors were

usefulness for getting a job

finding the subject interesting

own performance in the subject.

It would seem that girls who choose to drop physics are doing so because it does not seem relevant for any career they can envisage for themselves, it does not appeal to their interests, and they do not believe they are very good at it.

Even when the careers implications of subject choice are spelled out, the careers information available is usually prepared with either girls or boys in mind.  This means that traditionally male occupations are described in a way that appeals to boys, and vice versa.  Unfortunately this seems to be true even of new growth areas such as information technology and meteorology.

In the present climate, pupils need general information about growth areas, and most of these turn out to require a technological or scientific base e.g. paper technology, materials science generally, electronics, biochemistry, chemical engineering and accountancy.

For some ideas for showing girls how physics may be useful for future jobs they might consider, and for making physics more appealing to girls, see pp. 51-53 and 'Jobs that might appeal to 'feminine' interests' (pp. 57-63).

The third factor, pupils' perception of their own performance in physical science, operates differently for boys and for girls. Both sexes in GIST schools agreed that physics was 'difficult' and for girls there was a correlation between disliking physics and perceiving it as difficult. But the same did not hold true for boys who 'liked' physics even though they saw it as difficult.

The explanation for this sex difference may be that while girls consistently underrate their own ability, boys' characteristic tendency is to overrate theirs. Only 27 per cent of GIST girls compared with 41 per cent of the boys said they expected 'to do better than average' in school tests.

It is suggested that a slightly different approach should be employed by those counselling boys or girls about options, because of these sex differences in assumptions that pupils make about their own ability - see 'Good practice for options and careers', pp. 47-51.

## 2. Choosing between subjects

*Craft choices*

In many schools option systems are structured so that technical crafts and home economics are mutually exclusive. Often they appear in the same column as 'practical' or 'creative' subjects. The relationship between technical craft courses and the development of spatial and mathematical abilities and skills is rarely stressed, although for girls, with their lesser experience of technical and 'tinkering' activities, a course in CDT could be very useful.

Often children have already been siphoned out of the 'crafts' which are non-traditional for their sex by a rotational crafts time-table which operates only in the first or first and second year. If boys and girls are offered only a 'taster' course in the subject associated with the opposite sex, they are unlikely to opt back in against the tide when it comes to choices for the fourth year. Special request systems and taster courses seem to inhibit non-traditional choices. Teachers will often dissuade pupils from choices which they regard as 'frivolous', sometimes because of a fear of indiscipline or embarrassment. There is a danger here of being over-conservative, especially in relation to non-traditional options. There may be sound educational reasons for a non-traditional choice, yet in a national survey technical crafts and home economics/needlework teachers strongly associated their subjects with the 'careers' of engineering and house-wifery respectively. (Pratt, Bloomfield and Seale, 1984)

Technical craft courses are not simply the road to a job in engineering or even the basis for home hobbies. In a well conceived

CDT course children acquire the ability to communicate graphically, develop active design and problem-solving skills and learn how to assess and criticize manufactured products from the consumer's point of view.

## Science choices

Most schools encourage, and many require, their pupils to study at least one science. It would be to the advantage of girls if all pupils were required to study at least one <u>physical</u> science (i.e. physics or chemistry). If pupils drop these subjects in the fourth year it is very difficult to take them up again later on, but biology and arts subjects can often be started in the sixth form. Dropping physical science closes the door on many interesting and well-paid careers, and prevents children from keeping open a wide range of possibilities for the future.

## 3. Parental influence

Parents undoubtedly exert a strong influence on the subject choices girls and boys will make, and teachers may assume that parental opinion will always tend to the traditional. However parents are highly concerned about jobs and careers for their daughters as well as their sons. Some ways for schools and teachers to involve parents in these choices in a more positive way are suggested later, see Unit III, '3. Involving parents' (pp. 48-9).

## 4. Option booklets

It is not surprising that girls and boys avoid subjects which are presented as being more suitable for the opposite sex. Subject descriptions in option booklets sometimes use exclusive male or female pronouns, or link subjects with clearly masculine or feminine careers. Limitations on certain subject combinations often seem to be designed to channel girls and boys into sex-differentiated patterns of choice. Option booklets sometimes emphasize a web of links between woodwork or metalwork, technical drawing or CDT, physics and mathematics. If a girl is tentatively interested in taking one of these traditionally masculine subjects, she may be put off by the assumption that if you are going to do one you had better do them all.

## 5. Fear of being the 'odd one out'

Many pupils avoid choices which would make them the only girl or boy in the group. They think they would feel out of place and receive unwanted special treatment. Teachers may counsel pupils against taking a subject for the same reason. Special request arrangements reinforce the notion that pupils making an unusual choice will be particularly noticeable.

(Some of the material for this lecturette was originally distributed as part of a GIST booklet for teachers. The booklet, *GIST: Options and Careers*, by Judith Whyte, Alison Kelly, Barbara Smail and John Catton is still available from Manchester Polytechnic, 9A Didsbury Park, Didsbury, Manchester M20 OLK, price 60p. Please enclose SAE.)

Workshop activity 9

## Discussion of subject option patterns

These five points can form the basis for discussion activity, to be
followed up by consideration of some of the good practice ideas listed
in Unit III, part 3.  The following questions may be used as 'starters':

1.  What sort of preparation for options is available in my school?
    Are pupils advised of the broad career implications of dropping
    certain subjects?  Do counsellors tend to 'sell' their own
    subject?  Is there explicit discussion of so-called non-
    traditional choices?

2.  Do the craft departments have special 'mini-options' which
    channel girls and boys into the traditional craft subjects .
    before they reach third year?  Do craft departments discourage
    choices from girls or boys?  Do most girls drop physical sciences
    and opt for biology?  Has human biology become a subject for
    girls only?

3.  What information do parents receive from the school about option
    choice?  How are they involved in the process and at what stage?

4.  Does my school's option booklet imply by the use of exclusively
    male or female pronouns, or the linking of subjects with specific
    careers that they would be more suitable choices for girls/boys?
    Does the option system reinforce existing patterns of choice,
    making new combinations of subjects virtually impossible?

5.  What happens to the individual pupil who expresses an interest
    in a subject non-traditional for their sex?  What is the attitude
    of teachers to taking groups composed largely of one or other sex?

## III.  INTERVENTIONS AND GOOD PRACTICE

Unit III offers practical suggestions for ways teachers and schools may encourage girls to opt for physical science and technical crafts in the fourth year, and to consider occupations open to those with scientific or technical qualifications.

Useful additional material is available in two other pamphlets in this series, for science and craft teachers respectively.  (See Catton, 1985 and Smail, 1985.)

There are six resource ideas:

1.  *Fair Shares*, a 16-minute, colour video, dramatically reconstructs incidents observed in laboratories and workshops in GIST schools, and is intended as a starter for discussion of sex differences in classroom interaction.  The discussion notes for the video are reproduced here.  (The video is published by Drake Educational Associates, St Fagans Road, Fairwater, Cardiff CF5 3AE.)

2.  VISTA, the visiting women scientists and technologists scheme, which was one of the main interventions employed in GIST schools is described.  It suggests how teachers and schools in other areas may mount similar schemes.

3.  'Good practice for options and careers' outlines ways of making it easier for girls or boys to make subject choices which are non-traditional for their sex.

4.  'Girl-friendly teachers of science and technology' lists some good practice ideas for science and craft teachers to take up in the classroom.

5.  The observation schedule GISTOS is a simple tool designed with busy teachers in mind.  It can be used as a straightforward means of logging sex differences in classroom participation.  It may help science and craft teachers develop ways of increasing the level of participation by girls.

6.  A number of careers under various headings which correspond with schoolgirls' interests, but which require a scientific or technical base of qualifications are listed.  Existing career information could be refiled under these headings in order to encourage girls to consider careers which have traditionally been reserved for men. The lists may also be useful to teachers offering careers counselling, and to science and craft teachers discussing subject options with their pupils.

## 1. Notes on the video, 'Fair Shares'

The video *Fair Shares* is designed to stimulate discussion amongst teachers of science and craft, design and technology. Ideally it should be used in the context of school-based in-service training and presented by an informed member of the school's staff. These notes are intended to draw out some pointers for discussion, related to incidents shown in the video.

*Fair Shares* was made by third-year students at the School of Film and Television at Manchester Polytechnic in consultation with the Girls into Science and Technology (GIST) project. It was produced on a limited budget using competent teachers (who are not, however, professional actors) and schoolchildren.

### Interactions in the laboratory and the workshop

During the course of the project, some teachers invited members of the GIST team into their classrooms to observe the ways in which boys and girls interact in science and craft lessons. Observations in laboratories and workshops in the GIST schools showed:

boys frequently 'hog' resources such as safety goggles or drills, especially when these are in short supply;

boys usually gain more than their fair share of teacher time and attention;

girls can 'lose out' in science and technology partly because they never feel fully at home in areas perceived as 'boys' territory' and subjects stereotyped as 'masculine'.

However, observation also showed that teachers could manage with feedback from an observer to equalize the balance of interaction between girls and boys and their teachers.

Many of the incidents shown in the video were actually noted during these observations and have been dramatically reconstructed to provide a focus for teacher discussion of how girls can be encouraged to participate more fully in the learning activities and experiences of the science lab and the craft workshop.

### Scene: Outside the chemistry lab

In the video, girls and boys are shown crowding into the chemistry lab. In many of the action schools, GIST noted that girls and boys lined up separately before entering classes, and tended to sit in single-sex groups. This division by sex lays the basis for many later interactions.

Questions  :  Should teachers ask children to sit in mixed groups from the start of the first lesson in science/crafts?

What are the possible advantages and disadvantages of single-sex grouping in science and crafts?

## Scene: *Girls talking in class*

The girls are talking quite seriously about the topic of the lesson, but the teacher says 'Stop gossiping girls.'

Later on when some boys are having a chat which has nothing to do with the lesson, the teacher says 'Joe's table, stop debating.'

This seemingly minor difference in reaction to similar behaviour from boys and girls is an example of the different assumptions teachers often make about pupils according to their sex.

Questions : Which sex differences are 'real' and which are stereo-typed expectations?

How can language and terms of address affect pupils' views of a subject?

## Scene: *The safety goggles incident*

In a situation where resources are scarce, with only enough goggles for one person in each group to have a pair, the boys ignore the teacher's instructions. Before they have finished the writing assignment, the boys go to collect goggles, leaving the girls with one broken pair. This incident really happened in a GIST school, in a lesson on heating carbohydrates. The probationary teacher was not aware of the goggles incident until it was pointed out to him at the end of the lesson. He was unaware of the amount of time and temper lost when the boys 'hogged' resources. He said he did not think of the class as 'the boys' and 'the girls' - he just observed that some pupils seemed keener than others. In fact the 'keen' ones were all boys.

Questions : What are the effects of boys making first claim to resources in a subject already regarded as 'masculine'?

As teachers, do we reinforce different 'norms' of behaviour in the laboratory for girls and for boys?

## Scene: *Craft for boys only?*

In this scene, the boys tap impatiently while they wait for a girl to finish on the electric drill. Under pressure, she stops before she has properly completed the job in hand. GIST observation showed that this kind of incident is very typical, and often goes unnoticed by the teacher. Boys use a number of techniques, not always subtle, to make girls feel that the craft room is boys' territory.

Questions : What can teachers do to make girls and boys feel that craft, design and technology is a 'sex neutral' subject?

What can be done by teachers to ensure ordered and fair distribution and use of resources?

## Scene: *Stereotyped materials*

The video gives several examples of how stereotypes of female incompetence in books, posters and workshops help to build the 'masculine' image of science and technology.

Questions : What can craft/science teachers do to counter the effects of literature or visual aids which are sex biased?

How can teachers help girls to experience satisfaction from acquiring competence in, and control of, technical devices?

## Scene: *Girls learning to lose*

The scene in which the girl puts up her hand just too late, shows that part of the problem is the unwillingness of girls to make fools of themselves by giving the wrong answer, or on the other hand appearing to 'know it all'. As one schoolgirl put it, 'the boys jeer at you if you get the answer wrong, and call you a swot if you get it right.' (Peter Wilby, *Sunday Times*, 6 November 1983)

GIST observers found that teachers whose classroom management was firm, and who structured the opportunities for speaking or experimenting were more successful in getting girls to participate. A highly structured atmosphere does not mean an authoritarian teaching style, but a sympathetic and controlled environment in which girls will feel sufficiently confident and at ease to make their contribution felt.

Question : What classroom strategies will encourage girls' self-confidence and increase their ability and willingness to participate?

## Scene: *Good practice: specific questioning*

The biology teacher giving a lesson on lenses takes great care to ask questions of specific girls as well as boys. This ensures that just as many girls will answer questions. The male teacher then uses what he has in common with Vicky (wearing glasses) to draw out a fact about lenses. Both these techniques help to make girls feel 'at home' in an environment which has traditionally been regarded as masculine.

## Scene: *Good practice: providing space for girls*

In the following scene, after Sarah has held up the lens for the teacher to see, she begins to reply to the teacher's questions. She hesitates when a boy next to her tries to supply the answer. Without saying a word, the teacher rests his finger on the boy's shoulder, indicating that it is not yet his chance to speak. Sarah continues, and gets it right.

## Scene: *Classroom tasks*

In the workshop, the teacher breaks off from talking with some girls, to ask for some 'muscle' to move a bench. Two distinctly small boys arrive and prove unable to shift it. Boys are often asked to carry things, girls to take messages. This scene shows it can sometimes be appropriate to change things around a little.

*Scene: Options*

In the final scene, Cath is discussing option choices with her friends. They seem already to be destined for shop or office work, two of the occupations in which women are most likely to be employed. Automation and new technology will considerably affect job prospects in both these areas, but for girls at school, it is still difficult to choose a traditional 'boys' subject' without having to abandon the traditional 'girls' subjects' altogether. Friends and parents may discourage a non-traditional choice, but the school's influence can be crucial, especially in providing children with support to make a non-traditional choice.

'Fourteen is a most undesirable age for making subject choices, since non-academic reasons such as gender identity frequently predominate' (Milton Ormerod, in Kelly (ed.) (1981)

Questions : What can teachers do to support children who are considering non-traditional subject options?

What can the school do to ensure that timetabling and options information do not inadvertently discourage children from making choices which are non-traditional for their sex?

## 2.  The VISTA programme

Girls faced with option choice at 13 know science and technology are supposed to be boys' subjects. This is especially true if they are in a mixed school, when boys will have made them well aware of it. They are likely to believe that their choices are relatively free and may be unconscious of the pressures on them to choose biology, the arts and home economics. This is partly because there is no formal barrier to choosing the subjects; the hidden curriculum of expectations which structure girls' choices are usually only recognized with hindsight.

The GIST project devised a scheme called VISTA (Women Scientists and Technologists Visit Schools) which was designed to counter the usual assumptions about the jobs it is 'appropriate' for girls to aspire to. Women successfully employed in jobs requiring scientific and technical qualifications were recruited to visit classes and act as role models for the girls and non-traditional examples for the boys. The women were carefully briefed to present an aspect of their job which would be interesting to 12- and 13-year-olds, and which also had some relevance to parts of the lower-school science or crafts curriculum.

For instance when children were working on 'forces' a lecturer in anatomy talked about forces in the human arm. When they were learning about acids and alkalis a food technologist brought cakes made from cake mixes with incorrectly balanced baking powder, to show the use of pH measurements in the food industry. Learning to use a thermometer was linked to a talk by a gas engineer who demonstrated heat-sensitive crayons as one way of measuring temperatures. In craft, a supervisor from a small brass foundry brought along rough castings of brass 'tortoise' shaped doorstops and other decorative articles, to demonstrate finishing processes.  (For a list showing the range of occupations of the visitors, see Smail, 1985.)

Evaluation of the visits, by teachers' reports, and 'before' and 'after' questionnaires to the children, showed that they had been successful in modifying the stereotyped ideas of both boys and girls. Incidentally, the contact with people working in industry was considered valuable by the teachers and enjoyable by the pupils.  The boys showed as much interest as the girls, and their attitudes shifted towards greater liberalism, although a sex gap remained, with girls' ideas being more open than boys' about the suitable occupations for men and women.

The scheme was later extended to schools in the North West and is now run by a group of science teachers.  However, it would be feasible for a single school, authority or regional group to mount and run similar schemes.

The main features of VISTA which need to be kept in mind are as follows:

1.  The women should be carefully briefed beforehand, to ensure that they can make a lively and interesting presentation appropriate for the age group (i.e. not a sixth-form careers talk) and that they can communicate enthusiasm for the work they do.

2.  Someone with an intimate knowledge of the lower-school craft and science curricula should devise links with relevant aspects of the women's jobs and ensure that the visits take place in close liaison with the linked lessons.

3.  It is easier to enlist into the scheme graduate women scientists and engineers than to find women technicians and craftspeople.  Local employers, trade unions and the Women in Manual Trades Group* are a starting-point;  the Engineering Industries Training Board may be able to locate some female technicians and apprentices.  These women are often younger in age than scientists, and are therefore excellent role models for schoolgirls.  However they may lack the confidence to address a large group, and GIST found it useful to ask craftspeople to visit schools in groups of two or three, and to spend the bulk of the visit in practical demonstration, with questions and discussion arising naturally in a 'workshop' atmosphere.

4.  The value of visits is increased tremendously if teachers prepare the pupils well in advance, and follow up the visit not just with revision of the relevant lesson content, but with discussion of women in scientific and technical jobs.  Pupils may be enthused by talks and demonstrations, but they also need to know that their teachers are actively supportive of girls who want to follow in the visitors' footsteps.  For this reason it can be helpful to ask the women to say a little about themselves, how they came to choose this career, and what it is like to be a woman in a man's world.  They should also talk about how they have managed to combine their jobs and their family lives successfully, since many teenage girls still believe that the need for a job will end once they are married.

---

* 52-4  Featherstone Street, London EC1.

46

## 3. Good practice for options and careers

(Interventions indicated by an asterisk (*).)

### 1. Making the decision

Pupils and their parents should be helped to realize that option choices are important decisions which require a lot of thought. Pupils can be taught the skills of decision-making in general, and then as applied to option choices. The first part of the Careers Research and Advisory Centre's *Your Choice at 13+* (CRAC, 3rd edn, 1980)† has good pupil exercises on decision-making. This book is essential reading and reference material for everyone concerned with advising children on option choices. Two useful leaflets, for parents and children respectively, are 'Getting it Right Matters: a Parents' Guide to Subject Options for their Children' (EOC) and 'Third Year Choice' (for children on the importance of option choices in the third year, with guidelines on how the choice should be made) (Manchester Education Committee Careers Service).

Schools can:  *provide some practice in decision-making prior to option choice

*ensure that members of staff from a variety of subject backgrounds are involved in counselling pupils and that pupils are able to talk to several advisers.

Specific careers guidance is probably inappropriate at the end of the third year but it is important that pupils should be made aware of the possible implications of their subject choices, especially where these may result in cutting off entry to certain courses or careers. Children could also be encouraged to think about their future lifestyles and the possibility that choices which have not been traditional for their sex may be appropriate and fulfilling to them as individuals.

Even without special lesson time careers education may fit well into tutorial work or a programme of personal and social development.

### 2. Choosing between subjects

Many girls opt for biology alone because it seems to be the most 'human' science, or they think of being nurses. But biology on its own is much less useful than they realize. For nursing, biology (rather than human biology) and chemistry are preferred qualifications. Chemistry with biology can lead to 'socially useful' jobs in, for example, the food, brewing or agricultural industries. A number of traditionally female jobs such as dietetics, fashion design and production, floristry, hairdressing, laundry and dry cleaning, physiotherapy and radiography require or use science qualifications. In most cases a physical science is preferred or required. (See 'Careers that require or use scientific or technical qualifications', page 56.)

Many other occupations apart from nursing are directly or indirectly helpful to sick people. Dieticians, medical illustrators, laboratory

---

† The fifth edition is published as *Decisions at 13/14+: the Starting Point for Third-year Option Choices* (CRAC/Hobsons, Cambridge, 1985).

scientists and technicians and pharmacists† all work in hospitals and assist the health team. The whole of medicine is becoming increasingly technological, and jobs concerned with people's health almost always require scientific or technical qualifications. Where there is competition for entry to jobs, candidates with more than the minimum qualifications will be preferred. The same is true in other fields, for example primary-school teaching, where the growth of science in primary schools means that science specialists may be preferred in the future.

Girls can become interested in the wide range of jobs for which CDT, science or mathematics are useful qualifications, but the information needs to be provided in a way that takes account of their current interests. Engineering and industrial design are seen as 'men's work' but in tomorrow's world women will want to contribute too. It is mainly men that design kitchens, because they are the building technologists and architectural technicians. But the job might well appeal to a girl. Most children can be excited by the thought of contributing to the design and production of everyday things - telephones, children's toys, bicycles, cameras, food and drink or airports. If the approach is from this angle at first, girls can wait till later before deciding whether they want to go in for mechanical, chemical or civil engineering. A girl who is keen to work abroad probably does not know that agricultural engineering would provide the opportunity. Girls are traditionally keen on 'helping people', but usually unaware that the jobs of many engineers can involve the protection of operating personnel and problems of health and safety at work. Studying CDT at school may make it easier for girls to enter engineering where they may have to 'prove' themselves to potential employers in a way that boys do not.

* Encourage all pupils to study at least one physical science.

* Counsel girls, particularly high achieving girls, to continue with CDT.

## 3.   Involving parents

A national study of 'good practice' in implementing equal opportunities policies cites two schools which succeeded in consulting with parents to change stereotyped patterns of choice (Pratt et al., 1984).

The practice and experience of one school is particularly instructive. In formal consultative procedures with parents and employers policy was shaped to ensure all pupils study a biological and physical science to examination level; the aptitude and ability of pupils dictated whether they were examined in individual subjects or integrated science examinations. At the beginning of the consultative process there was opposition to compulsory physical science for girls, but it emerged that neither parents nor employers understood the relationship between modern science curricula and career prospects. On being shown the relevance of science programmes to a variety of careers the opposition disappeared.

The pattern was repeated in a case study of a single-sex girls' school when staff set out to confront traditional views by stressing the

† Details of qualifications required for each of these occupations appear in 'Jobs that appeal to 'feminine' interests', page 57.

connection between design and technology and the science curriculum.  In both cases educational policy, supported by professional neutrality, resulted in mechanisms providing equality of opportunity for girls and boys.

* The importance of physical science and CDT for girls could be stressed at parents' evenings.  Parents need to know:

    that girls are just as competent as boys in physical science or technical crafts;

    that physical science can help girls pursue their interests in other subjects, such as biology;

    that technical crafts can indirectly support girls' achievement in science, mathematics, control technology and other subjects;

    that physical science and technical qualifications are needed by girls for a number of courses and jobs they may later want to do.

    Above all, parents and children need to know, and believe, that staff in these traditionally 'masculine' departments now welcome girls.

    When the parents come into school girls can be demonstrating equipment and displaying work in these subjects.  Conversely boys should be encouraged to demonstrate their domestic skills when parents are present.

    * Discuss the importance of physical science and CDT for girls at parents' evenings.

    * Encourage pupils to demonstrate equipment and display work in non-traditional areas.

## 4.  Option booklets

For those parents who do not turn up at parents' evenings, the options booklet will be the main source of information when they help their children to make up their minds about option choices.

    Option booklets should always avoid language which suggests that subjects are more suitable for one sex than the other, or which implies that males are the norm, e.g. 'the pupil ... he ...', 'Man:  a course of Study'.

*    For subjects which are traditionally associated with one sex it may help to say explicitly in the option booklet that both sexes can take it, enjoy it and be good at it.  Teachers may not always be aware of the unofficial grapevine by which children come to believe that some subjects are reserved for one sex only.

*    Simple changes to the names of subjects (e.g. from dressmaking or needlework to tailoring, fabrics or textiles) may make them more attractive to pupils of the non-traditional sex.

    Pupils of the 'other' sex may also be encouraged or discouraged by the description of course content.  For example domestic science courses which focus on caring for the home and the family (i.e. traditional female roles) are unlikely to attract boys. If they mention caring for yourself, job opportunities (e.g. catering trade, machining) and work towards developing an understanding of people and their needs for food, clothing, shelter and satisfying personal relationships, more boys might enrol. In boys' schools where home economics is offered in a gender-free context it is often over-subscribed.

* Similarly, if the descriptions of CDT courses concentrated <u>less</u> on careers and more on practical skills which everyone needs, more girls might be attracted. Girls seem to prefer a design-based approach to technical crafts. Technical drawing could emphasize the need for
* neatness and indicate that the work is clean and light. Links can be made with graphics in advertising or the design of consumer products
* as well as with engineering. Typing should not be seen as leading straight to secretarial work; course descriptions could specifically mention the semi-conductor revolution, word processors, home computers
* and the trend for everyone to need keyboard skills.

* Very technical descriptions of course content (which seem to occur most frequently in physics, metalwork and technical drawing) are both unnecessary for pupils making their choice and intimidating to less self-confident pupils, mainly girls.

Most schools mention, quite rightly, the career implications of subjects in the options booklet. However care should be taken to
* include examples of both traditionally male and traditionally female jobs. For instance, if the importance of physics for engineering is mentioned, its usefulness for physiotherapy, veterinary work or growth areas such as materials science should also be stated.

   * Avoid all sex-typed language in option booklets

   * State that girls can take CDT subjects and boys can take domestic and commercial subjects

   * Make course descriptions more attractive to the non-traditional sex

   * Mention careers for which each subject is essential or preferred.

## 5. Fear of being alone

Many pupils avoid choices which would make them the only girl or boy in the group. They think they would feel out of place and receive unwanted special treatment.

Children considering non-traditional choices may not know of one another's existence. Teachers quite rightly advise pupils not to choose a subject just because their friends are doing it. * But for someone wavering over a non-traditional choice, the counsellor could mention the names of other pupils of the same sex who are also thinking of that subject. * Or they could be invited to talk to pupils taking non-traditional courses further up the school (or if necessary in other schools) so that they do not feel so isolated. In this way a tradition of girls taking CDT or boys taking domestic subjects can be built up within a school and there may be a 'snowball' effect as other less confident pupils join the non-traditional groups. This approach would also increase the genuine freedom of children to choose subjects when so many are still limited by their own fear of looking foolish in front of their peers.

* Feelings of isolation can also be combated by putting all pupils from the non-traditional sex into one teaching group (if there is more than one) so that they can form their own support groups in lessons.

* Aim to form groups of children considering non-traditional choices.


### 4. Girl-friendly teachers of science and technology

(Interventions indicated by an asterisk (*).)


A number of practical suggestions can be made to teachers who want to know how they can encourage girls to participate more fully in science or craft lessons. A fuller rationale for the suggestions can be found in two other pamphlets in this series written for science and craft teachers respectively by two members of the GIST team. (See Catton, 1985 and Smail, 1985.)

Four aspects of good practice can be outlined: 'girl-friendly' teachers are (1) aware of existing sex bias in materials, and develop ways of making their teaching resources more interesting to girls; (2) they appreciate that girls are more likely to develop an interest in science and technology if the starting-point is related to social and humanitarian applications of science and technology in everyday life; (3) their management of classroom interactions and practical work takes account of the different experiences and expectations girls and boys bring with them into the laboratory or craft workshop; and (4) they are explicit with pupils about their desire to encourage girls.


### 1. Countering sex bias in materials and resources

* Vet materials, worksheets, textbooks for sex bias.
* Adapt or add to those which appeal only or mostly to boys.
* Include work on women's scientific achievements alongside those of men.
* Make references to the usefulness and relevance of the content for women.
* Invite women scientists, technologists or craftswomen into lessons to discuss the work they do.
* If there are no female teachers of physics, chemistry or crafts, swop lessons occasionally with female science or domestic science staff, or ask the local teacher training institution to send you female physics/chemistry/CDT students on teaching practice.


### 2. Including social and human applications of science and technology

* When adapting materials or preparing your own, include applications of science and technology in areas which will interest girls because they appear traditionally feminine, e.g. stress science/technology in the home rather than in the factory, show how physics and chemistry can help us understand how the human body works, start from a concern with

health or with the environment when introducing new topics.

Do not make this an approach only used with girls; it can benefit boys who are equally interested, for instance, in human biology, and can emphasize the fact that science and technology are not exclusively masculine endeavours.

Domestic science CSE, O- and A-level courses are good places to start looking for ideas.

### 3. Classroom management

* Abandon the practice of asking general questions of the class and allowing the first hand up the right of reply. Address questions to specific children; this will force girls to answer questions rather than leaving it to the boys.

* If girls fail to reply, rephrase the question rather than passing it on to a boy.

* Encourage girls to be self-reliant and think things out for themselves. Do not do the work for them. Encourage boys to think ahead and plan logically before plunging into practical work.

* Choose girls to come out and do demonstrations : do not let them get away with being shy and retiring.

* Structure and monitor practical work carefully to ensure that resources and equipment are shared equally. From the first lesson, insist that girls and boys work together in mixed groups, or at least that groups of boys and girls work together on the same bench.

* Do not ask only boys to lift and carry, only girls to clean and service. But both sexes may need to be taught the best technique for an unfamiliar activity.

* Do not expect different standards from boys and girls. Praise girls for good ideas as well as neat work. Praise boys for neat work as well as good ideas.

* Deal sensitively with girls' (and boys') wrong answers and difficulties.

* Make it clear to children that they are welcome to stay behind after class or at lunch time to sort out problems. Girls may prefer a private chat to explaining their difficulties in front of the class.

### 4. Open encouragement

* Tell the pupils that you believe girls can do well in science/technical crafts and that many women will enjoy careers in science/technology.

* Ask the children to carry out a survey or find out how many girls/boys have taken physics/crafts in the fourth year. Discuss the possible reasons for the patterns they have found, discuss what they like/do not like about science/crafts.

* Explain why you think there have been fewer girls in science and

technology, and what you (and the school) are trying to do about the problem.
Explain why you have asked women visitors into the classroom, or displayed 'Women Scientists' posters.

* Make sure that girls understand the importance of the physical sciences and CDT for careers, and for personal satisfaction. In the third year they may be thinking of a 'feminine' career. Later they will have more opportunities to change their minds if they have continued with 'masculine' subjects.

* Finally, discuss strategies you have developed with other members of staff.

## 5.  GIST Observation Schedule (GISTOS)

### Notes for teachers on the use of GISTOS

At the beginning of each lesson observation, remember to count and make a note of the number of pupils of each sex who are present.

The GIST schedule has eight columns, allowing for notation of four categories of classroom behaviour:

### 1.  Teacher questions

T. asks B.Q./T. asks G.Q.:  teacher asks boy a question/teacher asks girl a question.

Tick appropriate column if the teacher clearly indicates a particular child.

### 2.  Pupil responses to questions

B.ans.Q./G.ans.Q.:  boy answers question/girl answers question.

Tick appropriate column if child answers teacher's question, whether question was directed at him/her or not.

Category 1 can show how many times the teacher directs questions to boys/girls.
Category 2 can show whether boys or girls are more likely to respond, and whether boys or girls are more likely to answer a question not directed at them, for example when a question was posed to the class in general, or when the pupil who was asked the question does not or cannot reply.

### 3.  Pupils' spontaneous comments

B.comm.spont./G.comm.spont.: boy comments spontaneously/girl comments spontaneously.

Tick if child asks a question, makes a statement or comments in any other way, without a specific question from teacher to child.

Responses to teachers' questions addressed to the class at large should be noted in Category 2 above.

T. helps B./T. helps G.:  teacher helps boy/teacher helps girl.

In practical work, tick when teacher stops and helps child.
(It is possible to indicate that the teacher's help was requested by
the child, by ticking Category 3 on the same line.)

Category 3 can show whether boys/girls are more likely to speak out
publicly in class.
Category 4 can be used in science, CDT or other classes with a
practical element, to show how many times teachers help girls or boys.

*Notes*

Use the 'notes' column at the right-hand side to note any examples of
sex-differentiated behaviour, for example when children spontaneously
form single-sex groupings, teacher says 'boys, come over here!', girls
take notes but boys do not, group of boys/girls regularly misbehaves,
etc.

Retain your observation sheet.

GIRLS INTO SCIENCE AND TECHNOLOGY (GIST) PROJECT

Classroom Observation Schedule

| NAME OF CLASS | | | DATE | | TIME | | | | NOTES |
|---|---|---|---|---|---|---|---|---|---|
| | | | | | | | | | |
| Name/Boy/Girl | T.asks B.Q. | B. ans.Q. | B.comm. spont. | T.asks G.Q. | G. ans.Q. | G.comm. spont. | T.helps B. | T.helps G. | |
| | | | | | | | | | |
| | | | | | | | | | |
| | | | | | | | | | |
| | | | | | | | | | |
| | | | | | | | | | |
| | | | | | | | | | |
| | | | | | | | | | |
| | | | | | | | | | |
| | | | | | | | | | |
| | | | | | | | | | |
| | | | | | | | | | |
| | | | | | | | | | |
| | | | | | | | | | |
| | | | | | | | | | |
| | | | | | | | | | |
| | | | | | | | | | |
| | | | | | | | | | |
| | | | | | | | | | |
| | | | | | | | | | |
| | | | | | | | | | |
| | | | | | | | | | |
| | | | | | | | | | |
| Raw numbers | | | | | | | | | |
| Percentages | | | | | | | | | |

55

Science and craft teachers are usually involved in informal counselling of pupils about subject options for the fourth year. It is often assumed that girls do not need to take physical science or craft subjects because there are no appropriate careers for them in these areas. Girls themselves at the age of 13 or 14 usually express interest in a very narrow range of stereotypically feminine occupations such as nursery nursing, hairdressing or teaching. They do not tend to see themselves as engineers. However there are many jobs other than engineering that require technical or scientific qualifications which might interest girls.

The following list indicates the wide range of occupations for which one or more science or technical qualifications would be desirable.

These jobs are then listed under categories based loosely on the sorts of career interests schoolgirls might express, interests in people, in the home, creative work or work with animals. It suggests a new way of looking at careers, somewhat different from the usual categorization of jobs as suitable for men or for women.

## 6. Careers that require or use scientific or technical qualifications
(The preferred science is given in brackets, where known.)

Agriculture
Air traffic control
Animals - work with (biology)
Archaeology (chemistry)
Architecture (all levels) (physics)
Armed forces (male and female, some branches) (chemistry and physics)
Audiology (biology and physics)
Baking
Bacteriology
Beauty therapy
Book-keeping
Brewing (chemistry)
Building (all levels)
Catering
Chemical industry (chemistry)
Chiropody
Computer hardware (physics)
Dairy technology (two sciences)
Dentist (biology, chemistry and physics)
Dental nurse/auxiliary (biology and one physical science)
Design - engineering, industrial
Dietetics (chemistry)
Doctor (biology, chemistry and physics)
Engineering (all levels) (physics, technical drawing)
Environmental health
Factory Inspectorate
Farming
Fashion design and production

Fish farming
Floristry
Food science/technology (two sciences)
Forensic science
Forestry
Hairdressing
Home economics
Horticulture
Housing management
Information technology
Laboratory assistant
Laundry and dry cleaning (chemistry and physics)
Leather technology (chemistry and one other science)
Marine biology
Materials science
Medical illustrator
Medical laboratory work (two sciences)
Metallurgy (chemistry and physics)
Meteorology (physics)
Microbiology (biology and chemistry)
Midwife
Motor mechanic
Museum work (chemistry)
Nursing (all levels) (biology and chemistry)
Nutrition
Occupational therapy
Optician (all levels) (physics and biology)

Osteopathy (biology and chemistry)
Paint technology (chemistry)
Patent work (physics)
Pharmacy, dispensing (all levels) (biology, chemistry and physics)
Photography (all levels)
Physiotherapy (chemistry and physics)
Petrochemical industry
Pilot
Plastics and rubber technology (chemistry and physics)
Poultry farming
Pottery, ceramics
Printing
Psychology

Radiography/radiotherapy (physics)
Remedial gymnast
Speech therapy
Surveying technician
Teaching (primary or secondary) (science)
Textile technology (two sciences)
Telecommunications (chemistry and physics
Trading standards officer
Vet (biology, chemistry and physics)
Water board
Weights and measures inspector (physics)

Adapted from *Your Choice at 13+* (CRAC)

Jobs that appeal to 'feminine' interests

This list is divided into five sections: 1. people's health; 2. meeting people/helping the public; 3. home and garden; 4. artistic/creative; 5. working with animals/interest in nature.

In each case the minimum required qualifications are given, plus any additional qualifications which may be preferred. For most of these jobs physical sciences are preferred to biological, and technical crafts to domestic. This is especially true for girls who are planning to enter a traditionally male field. Traditionally female jobs requiring no scientific or technical qualifications are not included.

*1. People's health* ('I want to help sick people')

| | |
|---|---|
| Ambulance cadet/driver | CSE passes. On the job training. Minimum age 21 |
| Audiology technician | Three O levels including biology and physics |
| Bacteriologist | Science O and A levels |
| Biochemist | Science O and A levels |
| Biochemistry technician | Mathematics and science O levels |
| Cardiology technician | Four O levels, including English, mathematics and two sciences |
| Chiropodist | Mathematics, English and science O levels plus at least one A level |
| Dentist | Science O and A levels, preferably physics, chemistry and biology |
| Dental auxiliary | Four O levels, including mathematics and science |
| Dental hygienist | Four O levels including English and science |
| Dental surgery assistant | Four O levels, English, mathematics and science preferred |

| | |
|---|---|
| Dental technician | Three or four O levels preferred. Mathematics and science most useful |
| Doctor | Science O and A levels, preferably physics, chemistry and biology |
| Environmental health officer | Three O levels and two As, including mathematics and two sciences |
| Factory inspector | O and A levels, sciences and mathematics most useful |
| Hospital domestic/ nursing auxiliary | No specific entrance requirements |
| Hospital porter | No specific entrance requirements |
| Medical illustrator/ photographer | Five O levels, including art and/or design. Mathematics, science and technical crafts useful |
| Medical lab scientist | Four O levels, including two sciences |
| Medical lab technician | Three grade 3 CSEs. Five O levels, including mathematics and physical sciences, preferred |
| Medical records work | Five O levels, including mathematics and English; or two O levels including mathematics (depending on entry level) |
| Nurse (RGN) | Three O levels, including English. Some hospitals require five academic O levels, including English and a science. Minimum age 18 |
| Optician | Science O and A levels, including physics and biology |
| Orthoptist | Five O levels, including mathematics and science |
| Osteopath | Three O and two A levels, sciences preferred |
| Pharmacist | O and A levels, including chemistry and mathematics, plus physics or biology |
| Pharmacy technician | Three O levels, chemistry preferred |
| Physiological measurement technician | Four O levels, including mathematics and physical science |
| Physiotherapist | Five O and one A level, including English and two sciences, physics and chemistry preferred |
| Radiographer | Two O and two A levels, including physics or mathematics; or three O levels including physics or mathematics plus one A level in science or mathematics |

2. *Meeting people/helping the public* ('I like meeting people'/'I want to do something that's useful to society')

| | |
|---|---|
| Accountant | Three O and two A levels, including English and A-level mathematics |

| | |
|---|---|
| Accountancy technician | Four O levels, including English and a numerate subject such as mathematics or principles of accounts |
| Bus driver | No specific entrance requirements. Evidence of mechnical knowledge useful e.g. CSEs in motor vehicle studies or other technical crafts |
| Butcher | No specific entrance requirements |
| Computing work | No rigid entrance requirements, but mathematics extremely useful for operators, programmers and systems analysts. Physics, electronics, control technology and CDT useful for dealing with computer hardware |
| Fuel and energy technologist | O and A levels in mathematics and physical science |
| Hairdresser | CSEs or O levels, particularly in science, chemistry preferred |
| Laundry, dyeing and dry cleaning | For TEC qualification minimum three grade 3 CSEs in mathematics, chemistry and English. Four O levels in English, mathematics, chemistry and physics preferred |
| Motor or garage mechanic | For apprenticeship, good base of CSEs, including mathematics, physical science and at least one technical craft. Plus evidence of relevant spare-time interests, e.g. electronics, mending motorbikes |
| Production engineer | At technician level, four O and one A level. Must include mathematics and physics, at least one to A level |
| Radio/TV service mechanic | Good base of CSEs, including mathematics, physical science and at least one technical craft. Evidence of relevant spare-time activities, e.g. computers, electronics |
| Taxi driver | See bus driver |
| Trading standards officer/ consumer advisor | Three O levels and two As, including mathematics, English and physics; or five O levels |
| Telephone engineer | Craft or technician entry. Mathematics, physical science and technical craft CSEs or O levels useful |
| Washing machine mechanic | See radio/TV service mechanic |

3. *Home and garden* ('I'm interested in how people live')

| | |
|---|---|
| Architectural technician | Three grade 3 CSEs including physical science and mathematics. Four O levels preferred |

| | |
|---|---|
| Architect | Three O levels including mathematics and science plus two A levels; mathematics often essential, art preferred |
| Bricklayer | CSE passes in mathematics, science and practical subjects such as metalwork and woodwork |
| Brewer | Five O and one A level, including science subjects, especially chemistry |
| Building technologist | Three O and one A level, including mathematics, physical science and English |
| Carpenter and joiner | CSE passes in mathematics, sciences and technical crafts |
| Clothing technologist | Five passes at O or A level, including mathematics, science and English |
| Electrician | CSE passes in mathematics, physical science and practical subjects such as metalwork and woodwork |
| Estate agent | Three O and two A levels, or five O levels |
| Gas fitter | CSE passes in mathematics, English and technical crafts |
| Gas engineer | Two A levels plus good base of O levels, including mathematics and physical sciences |
| Heating and ventilation worker | See bricklayer and building technologist |
| Housing manager | Three O and two A levels |
| Interior designer | Three O and two A levels; art, design and mathematics useful |
| Food technologist | CSEs, four O levels, one or two A levels, depending on level of entry. Chemistry, mathematics and one other science usually required |
| Gardener/horticulturalist | Entry at all levels. Chemistry desirable for TEC course. Four O levels, including mathematics plus physics or chemistry, two A levels |
| Glazier | CSE passes in mathematics, science and technical crafts |
| Home economist | Four O and two A levels. Chemistry most useful subject |
| Land surveyor | Mostly overseas work. Physics, mathematics and geography |
| Landscape architect | Three O and two A levels, including mathematics and science, history or geography |
| Materials scientist | A level mathematics, physics and chemistry |
| Market gardener | See gardener/horticulturalist |

| | |
|---|---|
| Packaging | A levels in science or technology |
| Painter and decorator, plasterer | CSE passes in mathematics, science and practical subjects such as woodwork or metalwork |
| Plumber | See electrician |
| Product designer | O levels in mathematics, sciences, art/design, CDT or technical crafts; or engineering degree plus post-graduate design course |
| Surveying technician | Four O levels including mathematics and science |
| Textile technology | Three grade 3 CSEs including mathematics and physical sciences |
| Tiler, thatcher | CSEs in mathematics, sciences and practical subjects such as woodwork and metalwork |
| Thermal insulation worker | See bricklayer |
| Town and country planner | O and A levels, including mathematics. Science or geography preferred. Some subjects not acceptable, e.g. biology, home economics, needlework, music |
| Upholsterer | Evidence of practical/scientific skills, e.g. CSE passes in technical craft and or physical sciences |

4. *Artistic/creative* ('I like art'/'I like the creative/practical subjects')

| | |
|---|---|
| Cabinet maker | CSEs in technical craft, mathematics and English plus evidence of interest and aptitude for an apprenticeship |
| Bookbinder | CSEs in English, mathematics, art and/or design, technical crafts preferred |
| Camera operator | For BBC technical assistant: three O levels in mathematics, physics and English and two A levels in mathematics and physics |
| Fashion designer | Technologist level: four O levels, including English, and mathematics or science, plus one A level |
| Film production | Five O levels and two A levels |
| Graphic design | Three CSE grade 3s including English and mathematics |
| Graphic reproduction | Mathematics, physics and chemistry preferred, technical drawing useful |
| Illustrator/artist | O and A levels including art or design; technical drawing useful |
| Industrial designer | Three grade 3 CSEs including mathematics and English, plus evidence of practical work. CDT or control technology useful |

| Jeweller, silversmith | Art college courses. CDT/metalwork/ design qualifications useful |
| --- | --- |
| Leather technologist | Chemistry or physics, biology and mathematics required for some courses, depending on level of entry |
| Musical instrument maker | Technical craft qualification useful, musical talent not essential |
| Photographer (advertising, fashion, film, industrial, medical, portrait, press, scientific) | Entry at various levels. Minimum three CSE grade 3 passes and evidence of practical work. Four O levels including mathematics, science and English, plus evidence of practical and imaginative ability. Technical crafts, physics, art and design all useful |
| Printer | Three grade 2 CSEs in English, mathematics and physical science. Four O levels preferred |
| Textile technologist | Three grade 3 CSEs including mathematics and physical sciences. Four O levels including mathematics, English and two science subjects often required |

5. *Working with animals/interest in nature* ('I'd like to work with animals'/'I'm interested in plants/nature')

| Agriculture/farming | CSE or O-level passes in English, mathematics and a science. For degree course, four O and one A level including mathematics or physics and chemistry |
| --- | --- |
| Animal nursing auxiliary | Four O-levels including English, and mathematics or science |
| Fish farming | No formal entrance requirements for water bailiffs. For fisheries management, biology degree requires good range of O levels including mathematics and a physical science, plus science A levels |
| Florist | No formal entrance requirements. Two O levels preferred, from English, biology, chemistry or art |
| Microbiologist | A levels in chemistry and either physics or biology |
| Meteorologist | A levels in mathematics and physics |
| Scientific officer (assistant) | Four O levels including English and mathematics or science. Mathematics and physics preferred |
| Vet | Three A-level sciences. Work experience on a farm or in a veterinary practice is useful |
| Zoologist | A-level chemistry and biology or zoology. Physics and/or mathematics sometimes also required |

Zoo work                              No formal entrance requirements.  CSE
                                      or O levels in biology, English and
                                      mathematics preferred


Sources:  *Your Choice at 13+* (CRAC, 1980), *Daily Telegraph Careers A-Z*,
          Manchester Careers Service.

Appendix:   ANSWERS TO WORKSHOP ACTIVITY 3 QUIZ

1.  What is the average completed family size in Britain today (i.e. number of children)?
    - [✓] 1.76
    - [ ] 2.2
    - [ ] 2.5

2.  What percentage of British households are made up of working husband, economically inactive wife and two dependent children?
    - [✓] 5%
    - [ ] 10%
    - [ ] 25%

3.  What is the average time taken out of employment by women to form a family?
    - [ ] 5 years
    - [✓] 7 years
    - [ ] 12 years

4.  What % of mothers of children aged 0-4 years are at work (F/T or P/T)?
    - [ ] 10%
    - [ ] 25%
    - [✓] 30%

5.  How many women workers in the UK in 1979?
    - [ ] 3 million
    - [✓] 10 million
    - [ ] 20 million

6.  What % of the labour force is female?
    - [ ] 29%
    - [✓] 40%
    - [ ] 50%

7.  What % of headteachers of secondary schools were women in 1975?
    - [✓] 20%
    - [ ] 30%
    - [ ] 40%

8.  What % of pupils entering for O-level physics in 1981 were girls?
    - [✓] 26%
    - [ ] 30%
    - [ ] 38%

9.  What % of pupils entering for O-level cookery in 1981 were boys?
    - [ ] 0.2%
    - [✓] 3%
    - [ ] 16%

10. Most women come back into the labour market after their youngest child starts school.  How many years between then and retirement age?
    - [ ] 10 years
    - [ ] 18 years
    - [✓] 25 years

(Information based on DES *Statistics of Education* and EOC fact card, 'The Fact about Women is ...')

## REFERENCES

Best, D.L. et al. (1977) 'Development of sex-trait stereotypes among young children in the United States, England, and Ireland', *Child Development*, 48(4), December, 1375-84.

Broverman, I.K. et al. (1970) 'Sex stereotypes and clinical judgments of mental health', *Journal of Consulting and Clinical Psychology*, 34(1), 1-7.

Catton, John (1985) *Ways and Means: the Craft, Design and Technology Education of Girls* (Schools Council Programme Pamphlets). Longman, York.

Coltheart, Max (1975) 'Sex and learning differences', *New Behaviour*, 1 May, pp. 54-7.

Davies, L. and Meighan, R. (1975) 'A review of schooling and sex roles with particular reference to the experience of girls in secondary schools', *Educational Review*, 27(3), 165-78.

DES (1981a) *The School Curriculum*. HMSO.

DES (1981b) *Girls and Science* (HMI Matters for Discussion series, No. 13). HMSO.

DES (1982) *Science Education in Schools: a Consultative Document*. HMSO, 1982.

DES/Welsh Office (1984) *Initial Teacher Training: Approval of Courses* (Circular Nos. 3/84 and 21/84).

Douglas, J.W.B. (1964) *The Home and the School: All Our Future*. Panther.

Douglas, J.W.B. and Cherry, N. (1977) 'Does sex make any difference?' *Times Educational Supplement*, 9 December.

Fennema, E. and Sherman, J. (1977) 'Sex related differences in maths achievement, spatial visualisation and affective factors', *American Education Research Journal*, 14(1), 51-71.

ILEA (1979) *Insight to Science*. Addison-Wesley.

Kelly, A. (ed.) (1981) *The Missing Half: Girls and Science Education*. Manchester University Press.

Kelly, A., Smail, B. and Whyte, J. (1981) *Initial GIST Survey: Results and Implications*. Manchester Polytechnic (mimeo).

Kelly, A., Whyte, J. and Smail, B. (1984) *Girls into Science and Technology: the Final Report*. GIST (mimeo). Available from Department of Sociology, University of Manchester for £1.00 plus large SAE.

Mee, A.J., Boyd, P. and Ritchie, D. (1971 and 1972) *Science for the 70s*. Heinemann Educational, Books 1 and 2.

Nuffield-Chelsea Curriculum Trust (1970) *Nuffield Combined Science*. Longman.

OPCS (1978) *General Household Survey 1976*. HMSO, tables 4, 5 and 2.2.

Payne, G., Hustler, D. and Cuff, T. (1984) *GIST or PIST: Teacher Perceptions of the Project 'Girls into Science and Technology'*. Manchester Polytechnic, mimeo.

Pratt, J., Bloomfield, J. and Seale, C. (1984) *Option Choice: a Question of Equal Opportunity*. NFER-Nelson Publishing.

Sears, R.R., Maccoby, E.E. and Levin, H. (1957) *Patterns of Child Rearing*. Harper & Row.

Sharma, S. and Meighan, R. (1980) 'Schooling and sex roles: the case of GCE 'O' level mathematics', *British Journal of Sociology of Education*, 1(2), 193-205.

Smail, B. (1985) *Girl-friendly Science: Avoiding Sex Bias in the Curriculum* (Schools Council Programme Pamphlets). Longman, York.

Spear, M.G. (1984) 'Sex bias in science teachers' ratings of work and pupil characteristics', *European Journal of Science Education*, 6(4), 369-77.

Whyte, Judith (1986) *Girls into Science and Technology: the Story of a Project*. Routledge & Kegan Paul.

Whyte, J., Deem, R., Kant, L. and Cruickshank, M. (eds) (1985) *Girl Friendly Schooling*. Methuen.

# FURTHER READING

Alic, M. *Hypatia's Heritage: a History of Women in Science from Antiquity to the End of the Nineteenth Century*. Women's Press, 1985.

Bone, Anne. *Girls and Girls-only Schools: a Review of the Evidence*. Equal Opportunities Commission, Manchester, 1983 (free).

Byrne, E.M. *Women and Education*. Tavistock, 1978.

Deem, R. (ed.) *Schooling for Women's Work*. Routledge & Kegan Paul, 1980.

Delamont, S. *Sex Roles and the School*. Methuen, 1980.

DES *Curricular Differences for Boys and Girls* (Education Survey 21). HMSO, 1975.

Eddowes, Muriel. *Humble Pi: the Mathematics Education of Girls* (Schools Council Programme Pamphlets). Longman, York, 1983.

EOC *A Guide to Equal Treatment of the Sexes in Career Materials*. Equal Opportunities Commission, Manchester, 1980 (10-page leaflet).

Grant, Martin. 'Craft, design and technology' in Whyld, J. (ed.) *Sexism in the Secondary Curriculum*. Harper & Row, 1983.

Hannon, V. *Ending Sex-stereotyping in Schools: a Sourcebook for School-based Teacher Workshops*. Equal Opportunities Commission, Manchester, revised edition, 1981.

Harding, J. *Switched off: the Science Education of Girls* (Schools Council Programme Pamphlets). Longman, York, 1981.

Marland, M. (ed.) *Sex Differentiation and Schooling*. Heinemann Educational, 1983.

Sayers, J. *Biological Politics: Feminist and Anti-feminist Perspectives*. Tavistock, 1982.

Smithers, A. and Collings, J. 'Co-education and science choice', *British Journal of Educational Studies*, XXX(3), October 1982, 313-28.

Spender, D. and Sarah, E. (eds) *Learning to Lose: Sexism and Education*. Women's Press, 1980.

Stanworth, M. *Gender and Schooling: a Study of Sexual Divisions in the Classroom* (Explorations in Feminism series). Hutchinson Education, 1983.

Taylor, Hazel (ed.) *Seeing is Believing: Teacher Investigations into Gender Differences in the Classroom*. Curriculum Development Support Unit, Brent, 1984.

Whyld, J. (ed.) *Sexism in the Secondary Curriculum*.  Harper & Row, 1983.

Whyte, J. 'Courses for teachers on sex differences and sex typing', *Journal of Education for Teaching*, 9(3), October 1983, 235-48.

Whyte, J.  'Observing sex stereotypes and interactions in the school lab and workshop', *Educational Review*, 36(1), February 1984, 75-86.

Useful addresses

Association for Science Education
College Lane
Hatfield
Herts AL10 9AA


Careers Research and Advisory Centre
Bateman Street
Cambridge


Equal Opportunities Commission
Overseas House
Quay Street
Manchester M3 3HN


GAMMA (Girls and Mathematics Association)
Secretary:  Susan Wright
Department of Teaching Studies
Polytechnic of North London
Prince of Wales Road
London NW5 3LB